from **Lamp** *to* **Laser**

from **Lamp** *to* **Laser**

THE STORY OF THE BLACKPOOL ILLUMINATIONS

Terry Regan
and
Andrew Hazlehurst

SKELTER
PUBLISHING

Copyright © 2004 Terry Regan and Andrew Hazlehurst
First published in 2004 by
Skelter Publishing LLP
3 Connaught Road
St Albans
Herts
AL3 5RX

www.skelterpublishing.com

A catalogue record for this book is available from the British Library

ISBN 0-9544573-2-3

This book was designed by Skelter Publishing LLP

Designed and typeset in Great Britain by Paul Barrett Book Production, Cambridge

Printed by Thanet Press Ltd, Margate, Kent

Cover pictures
Front top: Blackpool Council
Front bottom: Chris Parker

Contents

Foreword by Richard Ryan, Illuminations Manager

I am genuinely thrilled to be asked to write the foreword to this fascinating book about a subject so dear to my heart.

Illuminations have been my life's passion and it is with great pride that I invite you to read about the fascinating history of one of Europe's greatest tourist attractions.

The story of Blackpool Illuminations is all about people: the talented people who work on and have worked on the display in the past and those who still visit and enjoy them today.

To all of you I sincerely hope you enjoy the book and continue to enjoy the Illuminations for many more years to come!

Richard A. Ryan

Richard Ryan
MBA, MILE, AMIIE, DMS, I.ENG
Illuminations Manager
Blackpool Council
June 2004

About the authors

Terry Regan

Terry Regan, a happily married Blackpool man, is a graduate of Tyldesley School and the 'School Of Hard Knocks'. He and his wife Jean have six children, eight grandchildren, and two Scottie Dogs! By day he is a local builder, whilst in his spare time he is a writer/historian, having had several articles published at home and abroad, plus the odd TV and radio appearance. His particular interests centre on the history of Lancashire, especially Blackpool, with a bias towards the area's links to the American Civil War. He is presently writing a book concerning certain aspects of this war.

Andrew Hazlehurst

Andrew Hazlehurst has been visiting Blackpool to see the Illuminations for the last thirty years. In 1986 he attended the Illumination Department's Open Day which fuelled his enthusiasm for the annual spectacle. Ever since then, he has been a regular visitor to the open days and forged links with successive directors and managers. He is now one of the most knowledgeable people on the subject and was delighted to be approached to co-write the history of the Illuminations. Andrew is a school teacher and lives in Derbyshire.

Acknowledgements

I would like to thank the following for their help and support while preparing the book. My wife, Jean, along with my family; Gerry & Linda Wolstenholme; Ted Lightbown, Bob Dobson, Craig Fleming, and a host of other kind people too numerous to mention (not forgetting the publisher!).

Terry Regan
Blackpool, 2004.

Thanks are due to the following people for their help in producing this book. My wife Michelle and daughter Holly for their help and encouragement. Past and present Illuminations managers and directors: Richard Ryan, Keith Hall, Frank Hilton, Arnold Bennison and Arthur Elliott. The book would not have been possible without access to the amazing photograph archive at the Rigby Road Depot, a tribute to the foresight of Richard Ryan's predecessors. Thanks are also due to: Illuminations Designer (Graham Ogden); Blackpool Transport Services Limited (Brian Lindop); The Gazette, Blackpool (Terri Solomon); Blackpool Tourism Department (Mike Chadwick); and Illuminations FM (John Barnett). And last but not least, the Illuminations Department, for producing 'The Greatest Free Show on Earth'. If I have inadvertently missed anybody out, I apologise.

Andrew Hazlehurst
Glossop, 2004

The publishers would like to thank Blackpool Illuminations Manager Richard Ryan for his continuous help and support throughout this project. Without him, this book would not have been possible.

Unless otherwise stated, all photographs are reproduced with the kind permission of Blackpool Council.

Introduction

Enlightened times

Blackpool had at last become an incorporated borough during 1876. This was a very important year for the town, as it meant that for the first time it was in charge of its own destiny, and would no longer have to bow to outside political influence, apart from the Government. During the previous seventy or eighty years, the town had undergone a remarkable transformation, but that was to prove as nothing as its future was now firmly in the hands of its own citizens. Before long the city fathers would be applying to Parliament for an Improvement Act; prior to that, however, to celebrate the first anniversary of becoming a borough, the Council spent the princely sum of £25 on illuminating the facade of the Town Hall, by gaslight! Shades of things to come.

The Act was applied for during 1879, and subsequently approved by Parliament, paving the way for many wholesale improvements within the town, including the implementation of the world's first permanent illuminations on the Promenade. Apart from that very important item on the agenda, 1879 turned out to be a memorable year for several other reasons, amongst which was the launching of the paddle steamer Bickerstaffe, and the opening of the new St Johns public market. Several new hotels were built, including the recently finished Palatine Hotel on the Central Promenade. In conjunction with all this activity, large numbers of boarding houses had been erected, along with a variety of shops and business places, all lining the new streets.

The population of the town quickly grew, with more people than ever coming to live and to work there, as Blackpool actively sought to expand its boundaries. The ebb and flow of residents was staggering, which, added to the huge numbers of holidaymakers, almost caused the town to burst at the seams. Those crowds were even bigger than usual due to the proposed introduction of electric street lighting on the Promenade, an event that would almost certainly be the first in the whole world. The most amazing aspect of this was that Blackpool was only quite a small town, and had beaten several other larger towns and cities which later applied to Parliament with acts that would allow them to introduce electricity. The introduction of electric street lighting to Blackpool would be on a par with the introduction of piped water.

Indeed, 1879 was an electrifying year not only in Blackpool but throughout the world. Thomas Edison of the USA had produced what was claimed to be the first reliable incandescent light bulb (a claim later contested in court by Joseph Swan, of England, who also produced a similar lamp at almost the same time). These lamps quickly went on to revolutionise lighting, as did an even more powerful form of lighting, the electric arc lamp. Although Edison's and Swan's incandescent lamps would soon challenge the arc lamp for supremacy, both of these brilliant inventions would quickly find their way into the daily life of Blackpool, as the town was about to find out.

The sensational event was long anticipated by the many people who had heard on the grapevine that Blackpool was planning something extraordinary with electrical lighting, and when the Gas and Markets Committee of Blackpool Council advertised the date of the event (19th September 1879), visitors from all over Britain flocked to the town. The resort, which by now had become well used to experiencing new sensations, had never seen anything like the show it was about to stage; nor had many others. Reporters from national newspapers and journals attended the event, as did many industrial and scientific observers, some of whom came from overseas to witness the proceedings, which were about to be put into action with all due ceremony and celebration.

Many speculative reports were written prior to the display, and once the brilliant show was over, many fuller reports followed, especially in the trade journals of the day. One interesting example, from the Journal Of Gas Lighting, Water Supply & Sanitary Improvement of 23rd September 1879, provided a full description of the event:

"Favoured by the magnificent summer weather of the past week, Blackpool, the most popular watering-place in the North, has been en fete, and the inauguration of the illumination, by means of the electric light, of the promenade and the two piers has been marked with complete success.

In the Improvement Bill obtained during the past session of Parliament, power was granted to the Corporation to devote a sum of £5,000 to experimenting on electric lighting the amount of the loan to be repaid within a period of ten years. With the well-known enterprise that characterises the local authority and not withstanding the advanced period of the season, a Committee was appointed, Mr Challoner as Chairman, to make the necessary arrangements for an experiment in electric lighting on a very large scale, and Dr Siemens' patent dynamo-electric machine was the one used in producing the light.

The town's yard occupies a central situation, and here a wooden shed, 60 feet by 24 feet, has been erected. The dynamo-electric machines are eight in number, to produce as many lights, and are actuated by large pulleys on a main shaft, 4 inches in diameter, driven by two patent Robey engines, each of which is 16 horse-power nominal, and during the trials, when the machinery was in full operation, a total of 36 horse-power was indicated, the engines making 14 strokes per minute, with 75 lbs, steam pressure on the two boilers. The speed of the generators is 800 revolutions per minute.

There are eight lights in all, each estimated to have an illuminating power equal to 6000 sperms candles, or 48,000 candles in the whole. Six of the electric lamps are suspended from poles at a height of 60 feet from the ground, and are so arranged as to occupy three sides of a quadrangle or square, formed by the promenade and the two piers, the total length of the three sides being about 1,800 yards and the lamps averaging 320 yards distant apart, the remaining two lamps are fixed on the roof of the Prince of Wales Theatre, which fronts the promenade and is situated about midway between the two piers.

Movable parabolic reflectors are placed behind these two lamps, by means of which a beam of light can be projected in any direction. From the Siemens dynamo-electric machines in the towns yard to the farthest light on the south pier the wire is 1300 yards in length, and the distance carried to the nearest light is 250 yards. A separate leading wire is carried to each lamp, and one common return wire serves for the whole. All these wires are of copper, varying in the number of strands in each, and are insulated with gutta-percha covered by India-rubber.

At the commencement of the arrangements for the lighting, the whole of the wires were conveyed to the several lamps in 2 inch, and 3 inch, cast-iron main pipes laid underground; but during the unfavourable weather that prevailed in the earlier part of the month, the high tides swept the beach and promenade, covering the pipes in some places to a considerable depth, and filling them with salt water. This had the effect of destroying the insulation, and the consequence was the lighting entirely failed. I am of opinion, however, that the want of insulation was not so much due to the action of the water as to the iron of the pipes through which the wires were conveyed, and it will probably be found necessary, in future attempts of a similar kind, to insulate the wires by laying them underneath the surface of the ground in glass or glazed porcelain tubes.

This portion of the work had, therefore, to be commenced de novo, and it is due to those who had charge of the arrangements to say that, instead of being disheartened by the failure of their first attempt, they set about, with redoubled vigour, suspending the wires upon poles throughout the circuit. This was accomplished, and the whole of the work completed and in perfect order for the lighting, which commenced on Thursday evening last. The arrangements from the beginning have been under the charge of Mr Andrews, the representative of Messrs, Siemens, and Mr John Chew, the Gas Engineer to the Corporation, and these gentlemen may be congratulated on the result of their exertions.

Mr Siemens has also given personal attention to the work, and the Electric Lighting Committee at the Town Council have been indefatigable in their efforts. With the exception of a slight occasional fluctuation in one of the lamps, the lighting on Thursday and Friday, the opening lights was completely successful, the lights burning with remarkable steadiness. Had the lamps on the promenade been increased in number, and so placed nearer together, say at 200 yards apart, the illuminations would have been more uniform over the whole distance; but any disadvantage that arose from the width of the lights apart was more than compensated for by the effect which was produced by the parabolic reflectors. By judicious manipulation of these latter, magnificent beams of light were thrown in each direction alternately, the effect being scenic and sensational in the highest degree. In a spectacular sense, the electric light in Blackpool has proved a success.

The cost of the machinery and other the apparatus was originally estimated to reach £2,500; it will, however, probably amount to a considerably larger sum. But what of that? It may be said to have been wiped off already; Blackpool Aldermen and Town Councillors are very wise in their generation. The thing is a grand speculation, and pays. At this advanced season of the year Blackpool is usually empty of visitors. At present is full to repletion with 70,000 to 100,000 visitors. Not a room, or even a sofa, is to be had in any of the hotels, from the Imperial downwards, unless has been secured a fortnight beforehand. The lodging-houses, too, are overflowing, and excursion trains from all parts of the country are bringing thousands of trippers into the town, returning them after midnight, each day of the fete, to their respective destinations.

But what is the impression it produces upon the mind of the spectator in regard to its effect as a competitor of gas lighting? Simply this, that the latter rises higher and higher in esteem as a useful, easily managed, and ever present illuminator. Electricity may be the champagne of light of fete days, but coal gas is the Bass`s beer light of every-day life; and though the former is not to be despised on occasions, the latter is the wholesomer, not to mention the cheaper of the two, and what sensible people will prefer to use. It is a noteworthy and curious circumstance that every trial of electric lighting, however successful – and the greater the success the more I have the impression to which I am about to allude – only serves to prove its utter general impracticability as a general illuminant, and the impossibility of its ever, in the slightest degree, competing with the progress of gas lighting. If gas managers could only be permitted to take the trouble, and go to the expense of organising a display of the kind witnessed last week at the northern seaport, nothing would more contribute to prove the truth of the views I have expressed, and the utter folly and simplicity to gas shareholders who would timidly dispose of valuable property – about the most valuable in the country at the present hour – at a sacrifice, in fear of such a competitor."

This technical report is very interesting in that it shows that there were perhaps up to as many as 100,000 visitors in the town, all of whom were no doubt anxious to see the big switch on. We are told that every hotel and boarding house was full to overflowing and we are then more or less treated to a full technological background to the lights.

Now, whilst the writer of this article goes to great lengths to praise the lights, and to inform his readers of their virtuosity and quality, he then quickly suggests that they were little more than five-minute wonders, which could never compete with gas.

Perhaps the truth of the matter is that the writer, being business minded, immediately saw the true potential of arc lighting and maybe he foresaw it quickly displacing gas for the purpose of illumination. If that were so, then obviously he had a position to defend. He wasn't about to encourage gas company shareholders to start switching their funds into electricity generation. But he was wrong to say that electric lighting would never supplant gas as a form of illumination, although some buildings and theatres which now installed electric lighting also had gas lighting by way of a back up, just in case things went wrong.

The large excited crowds, having been treated to firework displays and mock sea-borne invasion and now having witnessed the implementation of the world's first permanent electric street lighting, were ecstatic. Blackpool had definitely never seen anything like this before.

Fresh air and fun

Shipwrecks, wind and weather apart, Blackpool is most famous for providing various forms of public entertainment, entertainment which comes in many different guises. These entertainments include the huge Tower buildings, and the sprawling Winter Gardens, both boasting magnificent ballrooms. There are the three Victorian piers, straddling the wide sandy beaches, flanked by the long Promenade. The Pleasure Beach amusement park, Golden Mile, the trams, several theatres and cinemas, golf courses, municipal park and a large zoo all add to the variety of entertainments on offer. Each plays its own part in making Blackpool's summer season so successful. But the crowning glory of the season is the staging of the spectacular Illuminations each autumn. They twinkle and glow along six miles of the Promenade, transforming the darkness into incandescent splendour, whilst drawing several million trippers into the town at a time of year when most rival holiday resorts have closed for the oncoming winter.

Envy, perhaps?

For many years, Blackpool has been accused of being a shallow, shabby town, that has little history, nor culture worthy of note. It is true that Blackpool may have few visible signs of anything historical, prior to the Victorian age, and accordingly the town cannot compete with places such as York, Lancaster, Oxford or Cambridge. But it doesn't pretend to. Blackpool has been in a state of flux ever since the town first tipped its hat towards tourism. Change has always been inevitable; so, inevitably, further change will come, as it always has done, at this terrific holiday resort.

There is history and culture to be found in and around the town if one looks for it. Celts, Romans, Saxons, Vikings and, later, the Norman invaders were all hereabouts, although there isn't much sign of this nowadays. Instead, the visitor sees the two main landmarks of the town: the Tower and the 'Big One' roller coaster at the Pleasure Beach, both structures being symbols of all that Blackpool stands for by way of innovation. The Tower epitomised more than one hundred years in the tourist industry by one local family, the Bickerstaffes, being built almost at the end of the Victorian era (an era that also saw the invention of the incandescent lamp, and the implementation of the arc light, both of which the town would embrace). The Big One was built approximately one hundred years later, at almost the very end of the Twentieth Century, signifying almost one hundred years' input into the holiday trade by another local family, the Thompsons. These two huge structures represent well over two centuries of tourism in a town where the winter population is in the region of 150,000, but the seasonal population of which can expand threefold.

In days of old

Before Blackpool became the huge resort of today, having either annexed or amalgamated with surrounding historical districts such as Marton and Bispham, the place was nothing more than two straggling hamlets: Upper Blackpool to the south, and Lower Blackpool to the north, both little more than a mile or so apart. These two distinct sections of the settlement were located along a narrow strip of almost primeval foreshore, replete with large sand dunes, and high shingle banks. The very small settlement was regarded as insignificant in early times, being just a tiny part of the ancient Manor of Layton with Warbreck, which eventually it was to subsume.

No one can be certain when settlers first came to this area, or when the hamlet of 'le Blackpoole' came into being, nor is it known when it acquired its name. It seems the name arose due to a rather dark peaty stream – anciently known as a *pull* – that ran through the area. There are a few early written references to the name le Poole, or le Pull, including those in a document connected to the Lord of the Manor of Layton, produced sometime after Easter 1416. According to the records of Bispham Parish, the first recorded birth of a child actually being born at Blackpool, occurred in 1602, when Ellen, daughter of Thomas Cowban of de Blackpoole (de Blackpoole being another name used for the town in this period), was baptised.

Great balls of fire!

As a point of interest, it is worth noting the baptism of yet another child during 1602. The child in question, Otto von Guerick, was born hundreds of miles away in Magdeburg, Germany. Although it wasn't obvious to anyone living at the time, by some strange quirk, fate had decreed that the life of this German child would eventually play an important role in the future prosperity of Blackpool. The reason for this is that as a scientist in adult life, von Guerick had studied the scientific treatise entitled '*De Magnete*', which had been written by the brilliant English scientist, William Gilbert, royal physician to Queen Elizabeth. As a result of this, von Geurick not only became the first person to demonstrate the practical use of the vacuum in action, he was the first person to invent a hand cranked device capable of generating electrical energy, and which in turn caused a large compressed sulphur globe to glow eerily in the dark. This was effectively a rudimentary light bulb. Both Gilbert and von Guerick were well aware, of course, that the ancient Greeks had discovered the magnetic properties of lodestone, and also that by stroking a piece of amber, static electricity could readily be created. This amazing power source was dubbed *Elektron* by those learned philosophers, without whom mankind may never have discovered the latent capabilities of electricity. It is also clear that without the discovery of magnetism by Gilbert, which in turn led to the discovery of the vacuum, and the generator of Von Guerick, there may have been no Blackpool Illuminations!

Although a man by the name of Whiteside is believed to have built a pair of cottages there circa 1501, the name 'Blackpool Town' didn't appear on a map until the mid 1700s. From its earliest beginnings Blackpool was just a small pastoral community, consisting of only a handful of rough dwellings, housing a couple of hundred souls, who were often bypassed by mainstream society. It had neither school, nor church.

Electrical connections

Over the years since the child Ellen was baptised at Bispham, the German von Guerick had become just the latest link in a long chain of scientists whose amazing electrical discoveries would come to change the world. Amongst these many and varied electrical scientists, who were now being increasingly referred to as 'electricians', there was a man called Francis Hauksbee, an assistant of Sir Isaac Newton. He concocted an amazing machine, which contained a large wheel, about which a glass globe whirled. As it was rubbed it became electrically charged, whereupon it crackled like miniature lightening, whilst also glowing with a strange blue-green light. This caused a sensation amongst those observing the spectacle.

A few years later a scientist called Gray showed that electricity could be conveyed down a glass tube, in much the same way that it now travels down a wire. He also demonstrated that the human body was a conductor of electricity. Many other experiments proved successful, including one in Germany where an inventor called Bose built a gigantic wheel, which when spun generated a massive static electrical charge. When this apparatus was connected to a female volunteer who, whilst sitting on an insulated seat, was kissed by a male volunteer, her lips flashed fire and her eyes almost glowed. This experiment was potentially very dangerous, as no one knew what the outcome might be.

A more important event was the chance discovery of the world's first crude battery, or capacitor, better known as the Leyden Jar (named after the town in Holland in which it was invented). This artefact was invented in 1746 by Pieter van Musschenbroek, a Dutch professor who was conducting experiments with electrically charged water placed in a glass jar, a silk thread and a metal gun barrel. Having informed a friend of his experiments, the friend then tried to replicate them; the results were almost fatal. He didn't strictly follow the advice, and succeeded in giving himself what was probably the first direct electrical shock. Musschenbroek's work led to the first crude battery, or capacitor.

Electricity was the 'hot topic' of the mid-1700s, so much so that many in authority were convinced that public demonstrations concerning electricity were dangerous. It was thought they might have a bad effect on the public, and therefore they should be shielded from such demonstrations. Worse, some of the inventors were accused of being sorcerers, and were threatened with being dealt with as such. Despite the warnings, experiments with electricity continued to produce results. Benjamin Franklin's very dangerous experiments with a kite acting as lightening conductor came along in 1752. Luckily he survived the experiments; others who attempted to emulate him were not so fortunate.

The times they are a changing!

By the time of Benjamin Franklin's extremely dangerous experiments involving the effects of lightning, and his co-signing of the Declaration of Independence during the American Revolution of 1776, a different, but not altogether less violent industrial revolution was taking place in Britain.

The village of Blackpool slowly began to feel the changes. Workers, who had so recently lived off the land, were now deserting the fields and were increasingly likely to be found working in the factories and in the towns. Due to their earning power being somewhat increased, a few intrepid Lancashire mill workers began to take an occasional trip to the seaside. They contrasted with a vastly larger intake of well educated gentry who, although not as easygoing as the factory hands, were apparently coming to take a dip in the sea. The number of visitors had now grown large enough to ensure that Blackpool would soon acquire its first purpose built hotel of any size. This hotel – Baileys – was built on an exposed seafront site during 1776 and still exists today, deep within the Hotel Metropole on Princess Parade. Prior to this, visitors would have been housed in lowly cottages or barns, such as the one converted by Ethart Whiteside some years earlier, or in Forshaws Inn, which is now the site of the Clifton Arms Hotel.

Workers, however, would have had little choice but to lodge in farm buildings, often mixing with the livestock, or if they were extremely lucky (or unlucky, depending on one's point of view) they may have been allowed into the small hovels that existed at the time. Here they were likely to be housed in overcrowded conditions that were so unsanitary that if they existed today there would be uproar. Often complete strangers had to share the same bed with the tenants, with sometimes as many as twelve to a bed! These people thought the experience worthwhile, though, simply because living conditions were much worse in the industrial towns than in the Blackpool hovels. It is said that inhabitants of Blackpool lived far longer than their counterparts in the polluted manufacturing towns, due to the abundance of fresh air on the coast. A dose of the bracing air was all that the weary visitor required in order to feel rejuvenated; this despite the rough accommodations, lacking even the most basic of amenities.

The incredible expanding village

As the village slowly grew and prospered, many of the inhabitants were not quite so dependant on garnering a living from the land as they had been. They now found themselves often catering to the needs of the growing bands of visitors, the majority of whom arrived by the now increasingly regular stagecoach services that came from as far away as Manchester and Leeds. Not all came by carriage though; a large number of wealthier people came on horseback, whilst many poorer souls walked to the coast, and back home again. This may well seem incredible to us in this day and age, but due to the very high cost of coach travel, walking was the only method of travel available to large sections of society then, just as it had been in the past. The stagecoach services, although very expensive and often unreliable, were helping the local economy boom as never before. And so it remained during the next generation, although advances in the utilisation of steam and electrical power were increasingly being brought to the fore. These advances appeared to have little effect in Blackpool, but things were slowly changing. By the dawn of the nineteenth century Blackpool was entering an era of expansion that was to propel it into the modern world. Change was taking place whether the locals knew it or not.

The Dawn of a new era

Steam was in the ascendancy in the factories and the cotton mills. It was driving the traction engines seen on the roads, and threshing machines on the farms. More importantly it was powering the locomotives which hauled the trains that were now appearing almost everywhere, consequently causing a revolution in travel.

Improvements in technology occurred almost on a daily basis. Coal-gas and paraffin oil were introduced, with more advances being achieved in the scientific and medical spheres, one branch of which was devoted to using electric shock treatment!

Limelight had been invented during the early 1800s by a man called Drummond. It was first used by the Ordnance Survey who utilised its extreme brightness to take

This advertisement from 1845 announces an omnibus service offering day trips to Blackpool, tempting would-be travellers with the prospect of 'sea bathing'.

measurements from one hill to another. Due to one of those strange factors that seem to have enabled Blackpool to take an early lead in illumination, we find that the first two places in Lancashire to be triangulated by the Ordnance Survey, were Beryl Hill at Warbreck in north Blackpool, and Beacon Fell in the Pennines. Later on, limelight was used extensively on the stage of Blackpool's theatres.

During the same period, Volta had perfected his battery, and in doing so had put an electricity supply within reach of many. There were many other notable achievements in the field, including that by William Sturgeon of Kirkby Lonsdale, who invented the electromagnet, which in turn allowed Michael Faraday to develop the first electric motor. The first arc lighting was invented by Sir Humphry Davy who, for some peculiar reason, didn't patent his idea.

By this time, engineering, ship building, and the cotton industry were going full tilt, as were the Lancashire coal mines, which were busy providing the fuel that enabled steam to be fully utilised, thus contributing to the economy of Britain, and increasingly, the economy of Blackpool. Victoria was on the throne, the British Empire throve; indeed, it was a brave new world, and Blackpool – having now found itself in the limelight – was looking forward to the future.

The arrival of the railway into Blackpool came a little later than some had hoped for. The town had, in fact, been receiving visitors by rail before rail actually arrived in the resort, the majority of whom were brought into the resort by horse drawn carriages from the nearest stations, situated in Fleetwood, and Poulton-Le-Fylde, both places having been connected to the rail network for some time. By 1846, the numbers of visitors wishing to visit Blackpool had grown enormously, so that it was inevitable that the town soon acquired its own railway station, connected via a branch line from Poulton. This station, later to be known as North Station, was built in Talbot Road and the opening event, on 29th April 1846, was treated with due pomp and ceremony. The station proved to be the catalyst for major expansion within the town and surrounding districts of the Fylde, many of which were now becoming dependant on the town's expansion.

Interest in electricity had taken the world by storm. Its importance cannot be overstated; as a talking point it beat even steam (if not as yet beating it as a motive power). This interest was most marked amongst the educated classes, and the industrialists, who were looking for new and improved methods of production and hence larger profits. Electricity promised vast improvement to many, but not everyone agreed. Some people still regarded it only as a form of amusement, whilst others actually feared it. The fact that electricity was seen as a source of entertainment was due to some of the 'electricians' who saw themselves not only as inventors, but also as showmen. In the best Blackpool tradition, they staged shows to excite the general public, whilst at the same time hoping to attract the attention of entrepreneurs. One such showman at the time was Henry Noad of London who, in 1844, produced a book entitled 'Lectures on Electricity'. This dealt with all the important electrical issues of the day, including detailing recent developments in such a manner as to arouse interest amongst the wider audience. The front cover of the book was a collage of electrical ideas, including a representation of the Wheatstone and Cooke electric telegraph, various batteries,

Looking north from Royal Hotel, circa 1836.

The cover of Henry Noad's 'Lectures of Electricity' (1844), the words of the title being spelled out by the sparks jumping from metallic foil.

Leyden Jars, magneto-electrical devices, an Armstrong hydro-electric generator, and several other up to date artefacts, including Franklins lightning rod. Also clearly visible were books and manuscripts by the world's leading authorities on matters electrical, and even a tank full of electric eels. The generator in the picture is shown producing electricity, which is then supplied via wires to strips of metallic foil, which spell out the book's title, as a result of which they are seen to glow profusely. A vision of things to come!

Around this period there was great interest in electric eels and many aquaria stocked the fish. Some allowed the public to handle them at their own risk. Blackpool had several aquariums at the time, and it is probable that the public here followed suit, just as they did when allowing quack medical practitioners to apply electrical devices to their person, allegedly to cure sickness or disease. Another development was the penny-in-the-slot electric shock machine, which enabled one to experience a shock at first hand. This was usually achieved by squeezing together a pair of metal grips, or by holding a metal knob protruding from the machine, whilst another person spun a generator. As far as we know there were no reports of death or serious injury occurring as a result, but these 'amusements' may have been potentially dangerous. The attendant fascination with electric shock lasted until well into the Twentieth Century, almost every penny arcade on the Promenade having several varieties of these strange and shocking devices.

Local families, early pioneers

Some of the population had the foresight that enabled them to take advantage of the opportunities that the coming of the railway, and later, electricity, would bring to the town. These people were mainly, but not exclusively, from old established Blackpool and Fylde families. Some had become wealthy several years earlier when they were allotted plots of land during the enclosure of the Layton Hawes, the massive common that stretched southwards for several miles towards Lytham. These included such families as the Banks, of whom Henry Banks was regarded by many as the 'Father' of Blackpool; then there were the Hulls, the Salthouses, the Bambers and the Butchers, several Cardwell families, members of the Bonny family, along with the Whitesides, the Craggs and the Walshes, to name just a few.

The Parkinsons were one of only a few families to seriously rival the Bickerstaffes in their achievements, as they too became major players during the development of the resort. Although once the opportunities that the town could offer had become apparent to all, the local pioneers were almost swamped by several waves of entrepreneurs, such as Serjenson, Holland, Caunce, Lumb, Sykes, and many dozens more. Such people possessed great acumen, tremendous foresight and determination. Such factors enabled them to develop Blackpool into the supreme holiday resort that it became, the results of which are still evident for all to see today.

The Golden Mile, home of tall stories

It wouldn't be untrue to suggest that some individuals and families did have a larger input into the success of Blackpool than others. There is a long list of contenders, although only a few individuals stand out above the rest. There is at least one family who deserve a great deal of credit for the success of Blackpool. The Bickerstaffes helped to create this town even before the coming of the railway, through their

Blackpool's North Pier in 1863.

industry and talent, bringing employment to many, and eventually endowing the resort with many entertainment facilities, the very pinnacle of which is Blackpool Tower.

In 1851, Robert Bickerstaffe, of Caunces Yard, Lower Blackpool, had built the Wellington Hotel on the former site of the village pinfold, having bought the site from the Cliftons of Lytham Hall. In later years the clan was involved in many other well known ventures that were usually successful, either operating solely on their own account, or often in conjunction with other old established local families including the Whitesides and Bonnys, the Parkinsons, and the Rushtons, many of whom were, or had been, fellow farmers, seafarers, and lifeboat crew members.

In later years, the Bickerstaffes were involved to a lesser or greater degree with the operation of all three piers, especially North (1863) and Central (1868, originally known as the South Pier and Jetty). The same family was heavily involved with Fairyland, the aptly named amusement arcade on central beach, built on the former site of Bonney's Bath House. They held interests in many other amusement arcades, whilst various members of the family were shareholders in local breweries, mineral water manufacturers, ice cream makers, wholesale food companies, cafes, public houses and restaurants.

The original Opera House Proscenium in the 1800s.

A Dynamic Duo

It was Sir John Bickerstaffe and his brother, Alderman Thomas, who were the mainstays of the Blackpool Tower Company, a company that had several holdings, and these not just in Blackpool and the Fylde. They also had interests at Belle Vue Gardens in Manchester and in the Isle of Man. Eventually the Tower Company owned the Grand Theatre, the Palace Theatre, previously known as The Alhambra, the Winter Gardens and Opera House and many other properties in the Fylde.

2 The true beginning

Almost from nothing the village had grown beyond recognition, due in part to the families mentioned in the previous chapter. This early progress saw Blackpool develop into a large town, and before long the town grew into a city, in all but name.

With incorporation came the first council, which included the Mayor, two aldermen and 16 ward councillors. It is unsurprising to state that the Bickerstaffes numbered amongst their ranks. It was shortly thereafter when Siemens came to town with his light show and the eight arc lamps lit the Promenade from 19th September 1879. And whilst the switching on of the lights was an amazing spectacle, it was intended to be permanent street lighting, rather than a novelty crowd puller. But it is this permanent feature – which due to its novelty becamce an attraction in itself – that would eventually lead to the annual Illuminations as we now know them. This is where our story really begins.

What the Devil!

Although most of the public welcomed electricity, some were actually in awe of it. The following poem written in dialect shows this clearly. This very descriptive piece, composed in 1882, commemorates several visits to the inaugural Blackpool lights:

Blackpool's Central Promenade with arc lamps, circa 1891.
(Ted Lightbown Collection)

"He wor agreeably supproist, on turning' out t'first neet, to see th'promenard an'booath pier yeds lit up by nine electhric leets, makin' it look as leet as day.

Joe wondert however they would get t'top o' those hee powes to leet 'em an' he went for three weeks hondrunnin to see 'em leeted.

At last, he wur rewarded by seeing 'aw th'nine lamps lit at once, without th'aid of lampleeter, but it took him so mich by supproise that he rusht off as hard as he could run to come and tell us that the divvil wur in th'electric leets and he'd turned lampleeeter.

He were undher that impresshun till we went to th' towns yard one neet an' seen 'em manifracthrin th' electricity at keeps t'lamps bruning'.

Two patent Roby engines, nearly laike a pair o'locomotives, wur busy turning' ten machines…"

An arc lamp opposite Blackpool's North Pier in 1893 with the Clifton Hotel in the background.
(Ted Lightbown Collection)

So, providing one can understand a little Lancashire dialect, it can be seen that some people viewed the introduction of electricity with more than a hint of suspicion, if not fear. These suspicions would soon be a thing of the past, however, and certainly did nothing to halt the progress of the new wonder power source, electricity. The minutes of the Council's Electricity Generation, Markets and Gas Committee show that, by 1889, the electric lighting was not only spreading across Blackpool, it was seen as a great opportunity.

The 28th November 1889 minutes make reference to Victoria Street, stating that "the chimney used in connection with the electric light urgently needs repairing, as does the dynamo machine at the electrical lighting station." On 29th November, references were made to the proposed introduction of electric street lighting in numerous locations, including, Church Street, Bank Hey Street, Princess street, and the Lower Walk, on the Promenade. Also mentioned as candidates to be lit are the Central Stores, and the two piers.

On 28th April 1890, the Committee resolved "that the electric lighting engine be repaired, and the poles on which the arc lights were installed should be re-painted, under direction of the gas manager." The same meeting saw the salary of Mr William Chew, Assistant Gas Manager, increase from £2, 6s, 2d a week, plus bonus of £25 per year, to a flat rate of £3, 0s, 0d. per week throughout the year. The 12th September meeting was told of numerous faults reported with the electric lighting engines, including great difficulty getting them to actually start up. The conclusion was that major repairs must be undertaken as a matter of great urgency.

We can observe from these notes that Blackpool was fast becoming a victim of its own success as far as the manufacture and supply of electricity was concerned, and before long a larger and more modern works would be a priority. Indeed, such a move was soon implemented when a new and larger generating station was opened at West Caroline Street, in the central area of the town. The works were opened with great ceremony by Lord Kelvin. Kelvin, the famous scientist whose name lives on today with the Kelvin scale, was very much interested in the study of electricity in all its forms and was largely responsible for the laying of several telecommunication cables across the Atlantic Ocean. As such he was a powerful figure, and the fact that Blackpool had persuaded a man of his calibre to open the works indicates the esteem he held for the town.

During the recent past the 'direct current generator' had been invented by Zenobe T. Gramme, who also invented the alternator, whilst during the late Nineteenth Century the world was introduced to the first rechargeable battery by Camille Faure, the transformer being invented by William Stanley in 1884. All these marvellous inventions would come to play a part in Blackpool's immediate future.

As a further encouraging sign of things to come, on 30th October 1891, the Gas and Markets Committee decided to extend the illuminating of the Promenade until New Year's Day. Normally the lights only shone when it was deemed absolutely necessary, partially due to the relatively high costs involved, so they would be switched off well before midnight. But this night they shone right into the New Year, resulting in a large number of people getting lit up in more ways than one on that historic New Years Eve.

The first electric tramway in Britain

What was to become Britain's first permanent public street electric tramway opened in Blackpool during September 1885, having been the brainchild of electrical engineer Michael Holroyd Smith. Apparently the idea for the trams came about by chance and was due to him visiting the Winter Gardens where there was a small experimental electric railway ride operating. It is said the company were having problems with the ride and Holroyd Smith offered some technical advice. During these conversations the idea of a street tramway car emerged and resulted in Holroyd Smith designing a scale model of a tramcar. This, in turn, led to the implementation of a plan that would see Blackpool provide the first practical electric street cars in the country, although Brighton and others had conducted trials of their own.

The new tramcar operated on a track covering some two miles or so along the Promenade, and was actually a joint effort between the tramway company and the Corporation of Blackpool. The early tramcars were powered via an underground conduit system that was doomed to failure from the word go. Not only did electricity leak from the conduits, but the wiring became heavily corroded due to the ingress of sand and seawater. On occasion the electricity failed completely and the tramcars had to be pulled by horse teams. Eventually, in 1892, the company sold out to the Council, which then became the sole operator of Britain's first municipal electric street tramway.

Not only did the Council buy out the shareholders of this tramway, it later also bought out the shares of the Blackpool to Fleetwood Tramway, which had been founded several years after the original.

The trams are still with us today, unlike the great American circus of Barnum and Bailey, which appeared in England during the 1890s, eventually arriving with a great fanfare into Blackpool. On arrival they set up their big top with its three rings, scores of exotic animals, clowns and acrobats, not to mention a host of sideshows that catered for every taste, on a field belonging to Watson's farm at South Shore. Barnum and Bailey pre-empted the arrival of the Pleasure Beach, which would be situated just a few hundred yards away, and to which the trams were destined to carry millions of passengers over the coming years.

Piers, deals, and big wheels

Blackpool's third seaside pier opened in 1893 and was to be known as the Victoria Pier in honour of the Queen. The construction of this latest and last pier caused a change of name at the existing South Pier, which henceforth became known as the Central Pier. As a result the Victoria Pier was later unofficially dubbed the South Pier, a name that has stuck ever since. Now the resort boasted three piers, North, South, and Central, a feat that has never been equalled by any other British seaside town.

The building of this latest pier owed much to the wealth created by cotton, coal, and brick manufacture in and around the small Lancashire mill town of Accrington, famous for its cotton mills and its bricks which feature greatly in the construction of many of Blackpool's largest and finest buildings, the Tower being but one example. Many of the pier shareholders hailed from this east Lancashire town, but not all were wealthy; some were just shrewd people who had worked hard in the mills, the coal mines, and in the brickyards and had managed to save some of their hard earned cash. Along with the business magnates, they pumped their cash into the building of the pier, which they not only regarded as their own property, but actually regarded it as a *de jure* extension of the town of Accrington, so much so that during Accrington wakes it seemed that the whole population of the town had descended onto Blackpool in order to take an afternoon stroll on "their" pier.

This same year also saw Blackpool Electricity Department's customers show a small increase to reach a total of thirty; although the engineer in charge, John

Blackpool's South Pier, formerly Victoria Pier, 1949.

Hesketh, now forecast a big rise in future usage. Meanwhile the electricity supply and tramways were now controlled by a joint department, having at last been divorced from the Gas and Markets Committee.

Tower power!

Of all the exciting events that were experienced during the development of Blackpool as a major seaside resort, few could ever hope to eclipse those that occurred during 1894. One saw the erection of the town's first purpose built hospital. The building, which was named Victoria Hospital in honour of the Queen, was erected on Whitegate Drive at Marton. This was a huge step forward as sick people had previously needed to be ferried to nearby towns for treatment.

A more alarming event that happened during this eventful year was the hurricane that hit the coast with reported wind speeds of up to 135 mph, possibly the highest wind speeds ever recorded here. Not only was much damage done to buildings within Blackpool and the Fylde district generally but, along the Lancashire and Cumbria coasts, many ships were wrecked.

On the entertainment front meanwhile Blackpool gained yet another theatre, the Grand, built on the site of several derelict shops on Church Street. The instigator of this project was Thomas Sergenson, a man well known in theatrical circles in Blackpool and other provincial centres. Having been employed at the Winter Gardens he now decided to build his own theatre and engaged the highly regarded architect Frank Matcham, who was involved in building many of the finest theatres in Britain. Matcham had worked on several other entertainment venues in Blackpool, including the Opera House. It seems that Matcham personally regarded his bijou Grand as the finest of them all, a sentiment echoed by many who patronise this lovely theatre even today.

Sadly, the little theatre was soon struggling for survival and within a decade was swallowed up by the Tower Company and became a part of that ever growing empire. To the credit of the Tower Company, they improved the place considerably and in doing so ensured its future success and continuity.

Blackpool Tower is nearing completion by 1893. Note the arc lamp standards. Note also the gas lamp opposite!

Undoubtedly though the main event of the year, quite possibly the event of any year, had to be the building of Blackpool Tower itself, literally the very pinnacle of Blackpool's career as a holiday resort and centre point of today's annual Illuminations.

This huge undertaking had actually been started several years earlier when, during 1889/91, the Standard Debenture Corporation Ltd of London bought several adjoining properties on the Promenade, including the Aquarium and Menagerie. The owners, The Blackpool Central Promenade Estate Company, which had sold out to Standard, were headed by Doctor Cocker, the first mayor of Blackpool, and a pretty shrewd operator by any standards. No doubt he came out on the right side financially; he usually did.

The aims of the Standard Company were to build a tower to rival the Eiffel Tower in Paris. Many designs were studied, including several that would have been higher than the original, but eventually the present design was settled upon. Plans were submitted accordingly and on 19th February 1891 the Blackpool Tower Company was registered with the appropriate authorities and £150,000 in £1 shares went on general sale to the public.

All was not plain sailing however as there was a lot of local opposition to the scheme, which many of its opponents were convinced would take their business, and as a result of this the company had trouble selling the shares. In fact, less than two thirds of the shares had been taken up, which looked like putting the scheme in jeopardy; that is, until John Bickerstaffe entered the fray. Not only did he put his money where his mouth was in buying a substantial amount of shares for himself, he also used his influence to charm several other prominent people to back the venture.

Thanks to the personal intervention of Bickerstaffe, the Tower was saved. Had his intervention not proven successful then the future of the town may have taken a completely path and who can say what might have happened as a result?

Blackpool Tower in its early stages of construction in 1892. Note that the original Aquarium and Menagerie are still in operation. For a fee of 6d, one could see the electric eels and other strange fish, though whether one could handle them is open to conjecture.

A long awaited event

The Tower was opened to the public on Whit Monday, May 14th, 1894, after three years of construction. During this time over five million bricks were laid by the skilled hands of those bricklayers who were in the employ of Cardwells, a local firm, whose roots hereabouts are lost in the mists of time. Two and a half thousand tons of steel and over ninety tons of cast iron went into the Tower's superstructure, as well as tons and tons of stonework and terracotta, plus acres of beautiful tiles. Plaster on the walls and ceilings weighed thousands of tons and the sheer amount of timber used throughout is almost incalculable, as are the incidentals such as pipe-work, electrical wiring, and the like.

Mention of wiring reminds us that the electrical age was by now well under way. The Tower employed electricity from the start, as the building possessed its own generating station, although, as one might expect, gas for lighting and heating was also installed. As a matter of fact, according to information supplied by local historian Ted Lightbown, seven Crossley gas engines powered the electric generators that

**Clown Charlie Cairoli
at the Tower Circus.**
(Daniel Potter/
www.charliecairoli.com)

were then sited in the basement, the total output of the engines being 1,000 brake horse power, whilst somewhere in the building there were sited at least two Robey steam engines, also supplying power to the huge building. On the 20th August, 1924, the Tower was hooked up to the Corporation electricity supply, which immediately caused five of the gas engines to be declared redundant, whilst the remaining two that drove the pumps followed later that year. One peculiarity regarding the Tower lifts is worth mentioning, as it seems that from the outset the gas engines couldn't provide enough electrical energy to operate them. According to some reports the lifts were only operated by electricity as far as the 85ft level, from where a hydraulic system took over.

The Tower and its amazing features were now firmly entrenched in the Blackpool holiday scene. Amongst those features were the lovely ballroom and the fantastic circus with its rise and fall flooring in the ring, which was often lowered and subsequently flooded to provide exciting water shows featuring clowns and various acts. The early entertainers at this venue are legend, whether human or otherwise. One of the most amusing acts amongst many must have been the cricket playing elephants, and quite possibly one of the biggest names to have played there in its early years was a man called WC Fields, later to find fame in Hollywood.

Since those early years many performers have found their way to the Tower, although the name that is perhaps almost synonymous with the famous venue has to be the one and only Charlie Cairoli, the lovable clown extraordinaire.

Kaleidoscopic dynamos

1895/6 saw yet another frenetic period in the life of Blackpool. On the weather front, more storms wreaked further damage to the sea wall and Promenade, whilst on the entertainment front the town witnessed another theatre being built, a big wheel constructed and the massive and beautiful Empress Ballroom being built on an adjacent part of the Winter Gardens site. In unison with all this activity there was the usual frenzied activity in the private building trade, as dozens of new streets were laid out and new estates were built in their wake, in addition to row upon row of

**Looking south from
Blackpool's Central Pier
in 1896. The sea defences
of the time provided little
protection against high
tides.**

boarding houses, shops, and several large hotels. A new town hall was also about to be built at Talbot Square, to replace the original that was by now in imminent danger of collapse and was only being kept upright by massive timber props.

The aforementioned theatre, the Princes Theatre – shortly to be renamed the Empire – was actually designed as yet another circus. After a short space of time this venture failed and the theatre evolved in its place. However, this business venture almost immediately collapsed for the simple reason that there were now too many such venues, playing to too few customers. It was only a shrewd move by the management that saved the day when they poached J R Huddlestone from the Winter Gardens Company. He duly arrived with a long and successful track record that included putting the Gardens themselves back into the black after several disastrous seasons. Huddlestone had been treated rather like the Pied Piper by the Gardens' management, for they promised him a huge bonus if he saved them from the risk of bankruptcy; when he did, they reneged on the deal.

The Empress Ballroom at the Winter Gardens.

A couple of very successful seasons at the Empire, which saw Huddlestone secure the services of the cream of British and foreign music hall stars, actors and musicians, soon had the Winter Gardens Company knocking on his door with a vastly improved offer, and his long overdue bonus to boot.

Several years passed after Huddlestone's departure and the Empire underwent another change of name, as it now became the Hippodrome Theatre, a name it stuck with until well after the Second World War. It was later converted into a cinema/theatre and eventually became, reputedly, Europe's largest night club. Goodness knows what the old stagers such as Bransby Williams would have made of this; although he might have been dismayed, the present venue might well appeal to one of his co-stars. She was a performer called La Belle Rose, a lithe dancer who did 'picturesque' dances on a large illuminated rolling ball that, according to contemporary newspaper reports, were "*kaleidoscopic in their colourful electrical effects*". Electricity had by now reached the stage where it was used to great effect.

Absolutely the largest undertaking of 1895/6 without a doubt was the erection of the Big Wheel on the Winter Gardens site abutting Adelaide Street. Naturally, this attraction was not without a certain amount of melodrama, as the designer was sued for infringing the design patent of the original Ferris wheel built in Chicago, USA. This probably added spice to the event, and surely captured the attention of the British public; and as they say in show business, "*there is no such thing as bad publicity*".

The Gigantic Wheel, as it was known originally, was designed to be 230 feet tall and weighed in the region of 100 tons. The axle alone, which was reputed to be the largest casting the world had then ever seen, weighed in at well over 30 tons. The Wheel's operators advertised their ride as "*The most beautiful example of ironwork in the North of England*", whilst affording "*the finest panorama in the world*", a panorama so breathtaking that "*artists should paint it*". These sweeping statements must have aroused some interesting comments at the nearby Tower. There were 30 large carriages on the Wheel, each holding up to thirty passengers paying sixpence a

For many years the Tower and Big Wheel were the most prominent features on the Blackpool skyline. The Big Wheel stood from 1896 until 1929. This view is from Adelaide Street looking west.

(Andrew Hazlehurst Collection)

time, and the whole thing presented a wonderful scene to onlookers, especially at night when the carriages and the perimeter of the Wheel were spectacularly illuminated. For many years a trip up the Wheel was seen as a must by visitors and residents alike. However, by 1928 the operation was losing money fast, as the wheel was judged to revolve too slowly, and so it was decided that the attraction be scrapped.

In the field of electrical activity, much was going on in this period. The science and industry surrounding electrical power was improving its performance in leaps and bounds. Electropathy as a form of medical treatment was still being advertised in the local newspapers and indeed, although there were many quack doctors operating within this sphere, there were claimed to be certain proven benefits from electrical treatment, but only if applied by the real experts.

The incandescent light bulb was now in evidence almost everywhere, especially in commercial buildings and in places of entertainment. Many of Blackpool's leading establishments featured light shows and other forms of electrical entertainment took place. The Winter Gardens announced plans for possibly the world's biggest illuminated sign; this sign would adorn the newly formed arched entrance to the amusement park. It was to be fabricated from opal glass with a ruby red glass background, all of which was to be backlit in such a manner that it could be seen from anywhere on the Promenade, from each of the piers, and even from the decks of the steamers that plied for hire on the high seas. No doubt the effect must have been stunning to all who saw it for the first time. What a brilliant new form of advertising this was to be, and yet another electrical triumph for the company which was now operating its own generating station that had a similar output to that of the Council's plant, but was producing electricity at roughly one third of the cost of that produced by the Corporation. It was stated at the time that of all the local authorities and companies now generating electricity, the only place in Britain that could equal the Winter Gardens on price was Edinburgh.

The Winter Gardens generating station was a formidable affair, as this excerpt from an article in the 'Electricity' magazine of December 1889 shows:

"The station is situated to the right of the Empress ballroom, and is supplied with steam from four boilers, three of which are made by Messrs Tinker, of Hyde, each capable of evaporating 5000lbs of water per hour; a fourth boiler by Babcock and Wilson was capable of evaporating 8000lbs of water per hour…the pumps supplying these boilers are of the Watson type…in the engineering room there are three compound Bellis high-speed engines, each of 300 bhp…there is also one 100bhp compound engine of 140lbs steam pressure. The three large engines are linked to direct current dynamos manufactured by Holmes and co of

The powerhouse at the Winter Gardens, 1899.
(Terry Regan Collection)

Newcastle, the output of each is 1,750 Amperes at 110 volts. The small engine is linked to a two-pole direct current dynamo which is capable of an output of some 60 kilowatts…this machine can either supply current to the bus bars, or supply current to the battery of 60, 17 plate Prichett and Gold accumulators. The current from the dynamos is carried to the bus bars on the main switchboard …that then conveys the current to various portions of the Gardens complex, via twelve mains."

It is quite obvious that the above was a very complex undertaking and also a very expensive operation indeed, even for such an enterprising and go ahead private company as the Winter Gardens!

Meanwhile, there was a new Chief Electrical Engineer by the name of Robert Quinn at Blackpool Council. The official appointment of this man was quite a feather in the cap for the Council which, having enticed him to leave the employ of one of its oldest and keenest of competitors, Brighton Council, were delighted with their capture.

Enterprise for a new century

The years in the run up to the Twentieth Century again saw much enterprise and progress that came in many shapes and forms. During this period, Blackpool saw the Diamond Jubilee of Queen Victoria, which was duly celebrated all over the town. As with the rest of the country, many local establishments went overboard with displays. Some, notably the Tower and the Raikes Hall Pleasure Gardens, presented highly coloured illuminations. The display at Raikes Hall was particularly spectacular, with its illuminated fountains shooting jets of coloured water high into the night sky, not to mention the three specially illuminated tram cars that ran on the Promenade.

The Alhambra Theatre was opened during 1899 on the site of the Prince of Wales Theatre and again, according to records on the subject, it too had its own electricity supply from the outset. This time, though, the generators were driven by two Lancashire steam boilers, driving compound high pressure engines with a total combined output of about 400 BHP.

Eventually in 1903 the Theatre, which had struggled from the outset, was acquired by the Tower Company. Having paid a reputed £140,000 for the building, they spent a large amount of money revamping the venue, which they then renamed the Palace Theatre. It later became famous for its variety acts, these continuing right up until its

The Palace Theatre, circa in 1904, formerly the Alhambra, prior to its takeover by the Tower Company.

eventual closure in the 1960s. The cream of the world's entertainers strode the stage at this late lamented palace of pleasure, the like of which the town will never see again.

During that same year the Central Railway Station was completely re-built. Now it was a much larger building with several more platforms, which were desperately needed to accommodate the ever growing traffic. Records show that during the busiest weeks of the season the queues of trains wishing to enter the station backed up all the way to Kirkham, and sometimes almost into the outskirts of Preston, fifteen miles distant.

Whilst all this new development was taking place at the turn of the century, Blackpool was in imminent danger of losing one of its most popular destinations. The Raikes Hall Pleasure Gardens were now almost derelict and the days of popular light entertainment there were numbered. It was the builders, rather than performers, who were now seen waiting in the wings, licking their lips in anticipation of fat profits to come.

Golden opportunities

By the turn of the century, however, the Golden Mile, as it became known, was well established on the landward side of the Promenade known then as South Beach (later renamed Central Beach). The reasons for the existence of the Golden Mile were actually quite simple. During the mid 1800s the Council had issued an edict that most of those who sold merchandise, or provided questionable services on the sands, were forthwith banned from such activities. Boatmen, donkey operators, and Punch and Judy men were amongst the very few to escape the ban that saw the beach rid of many other operators. However this byelaw did not see off some of these very determined and cunning people, for they merely offered to pay rent in order to use the gardens of the boarding houses and other establishments that faced the sea. Soon business was booming as never before as now these opportunists didn't have to dodge the tides (except on stormy days, that is). So much money was generated there that the name Golden Mile soon became a watchword for the area, even though the stretch of promenade in question was only a little over a half a mile long.

Below left: **The Palace Building.**
(Andrew Hazlehurst Collection)

Below right: **View from Blackpool Tower in 1903; note there is no Princess Parade!**
(Andrew Hazlehurst Collection)

Long Live the King! 4

The dawn of the Twentieth Century was a turning point in history if ever there was one. In many ways, 1901 was a sad year. Queen Victoria had died and the nation and empire was in a deep state of mourning. Meanwhile, the Boer War was in full swing in southern Africa, whilst in America a mad man had shot President McKinley. In Sweden, Alfred Nobel – the inventor of Dynamite – inaugurated the Nobel Peace prize. The season continued as usual though and visitors still enjoyed their trips to the resort, whilst the ever voracious builders continued with their many developments. Dame Nellie Melba appeared in concert at the Winter Gardens, whilst the almost equally famous Clara Butt was also appearing in town.

On 26th June 1902, King Edward VII was crowned and celebrations were in full swing everywhere. The Promenade was decorated from one end to the other with bunting and flags in abundance. Floral displays were everywhere, street parties were held all over the town, and the Promenade saw many illuminated displays that ranged from festoons of coloured electric lamps, to large and imposing illuminated features at the Town Hall. These consisted of motifs depicting a crown, and of the Union Flag as well as several star motifs. Co-incidentally the town's crest was also displayed, but in this instance the illumination was provided by gas jets magnified by glass reflectors. It seemed the belts and braces mode of thinking was still in evidence.

The Tower was also displaying a gigantic illuminated royal cipher sited halfway up the structure on the seaward side, whilst other prominent buildings such as the Alhambra were also displaying electric light features. The most striking of these was perhaps that of the Big Wheel, which was clearly outlined with electric lamps, making it visible from almost every point in the town and the surrounding countryside. At the same site the dome of the Opera House was brilliantly lit and made a striking feature, as did the Winter Gardens with its illuminated sign. All in all these displays were the most serious attempt yet at a unified illuminated display.

This was a very busy year for the resort; droves of day trippers and staying customers in hundreds of trains descended onto the town's railway stations each week. The beaches were packed tightly and everyone was doing a roaring trade, including the ever growing numbers of motor charabanc operators.

Blackpool was in the news again; it seemed that every newspaper and magazine in the land produced articles on the booming resort. One article published

The Tower, Winter Gardens and other entertainment buildings on Blackpool's Promenade present a unified illuminated display in 1903.
(Andrew Hazlehurst Collection)

in the Daily News gave a detailed picture of the thronging promenade and beach life of the day. The writer gave a very detailed account of the theatres and sideshows and of the itinerant traders and salesmen that were seen everywhere. These included quack doctors, fortune tellers, weight guessers, phrenologists, one man band musicians, ice cream and rock sellers along with many others too numerous to mention. Quite like old times really.

The one thing which intrigued the writer above all was the sheer number of 'mock auction' rooms on and around the Promenade. He went on to give a detailed account of the rip-off merchants who ran these crooked establishments, and his graphic stories concerning the "mugs" (as he put it) who were attracted to these places expecting a bargain, only to be duped in the process, are a gem.

Many new electrical innovations were being marketed almost as fast as industry could produce them, and one such feature was introduced at the Winter Gardens where, in true Blackpool fashion, controversy reared its head once more.

The general manager, J R Huddlestone, now working in relationship with John Tiller and his famous dance troupe, had visited an international exposition at the Moulin Rouge in Paris. The Tiller girls were appearing at that famous venue when Huddlestone struck a deal to buy a switchback railway known as 'Les Montagnes Russes' (or, The Russian Mountains) from the exhibition grounds, with the intention of exporting it to England. The deal was done and the ride brought to Blackpool, where it was erected in the shadow of the Big Wheel.

Immediately, the huge ride with its brilliant array of nocturnal illuminations caused a sensation, but not the sensation that the new owners were looking for. Instead they now found themselves on the wrong end of things with the hoteliers in Adelaide Street and other nearby streets, who were loudly complaining that their clientele couldn't get to sleep at night due to the noise and the bright lights on the popular ride. As a result the Council got involved and threatened the operators with an injunction and closure. To pacify the Council and the hoteliers the ride was stripped down and re-erected on another part of the site. Eventually a compromise was reached, with the ride only operating during the day.

A pleasant day on the exclusive Claremont Estate at Blackpool's North Shore in 1904.

(Andrew Hazlehurst Collection)

A view of bustling Blackpool in 1905, showing the town's two major landmarks, the Tower and Big Wheel.
(Andrew Hazlehurst Collection)

1903 came and went in the usual flamboyant manner. A huge storm wracked the coast, causing serious damage up and down the town. The town was, as usual, very busy, with big name stars featuring in all its theatres, amongst whom was the great American Marching Band, directed by Sousa at the Winter Gardens. The Winter Gardens buildings featured yet more illuminated displays, with floodlighting in abundance. The Tower and the Palace (formerly the Alhambra) were now owned by the same company, each building having had its own independent electrical generating station. The two systems were now joined together, thus enabling the company to switch off one of the generators during quiet periods, and as a result supplying both buildings with electric power from one generator alone.

Stars on stage, star status for the town

At the Winter Gardens the highlight of 1904 was the appearance of the great Australian star, Dame Nellie Melba, one of several she made in this era. This appearance was followed closely by another lady singer almost as famous. Madame Albini was one of the highest paid female performers in the world and her sublime performances, aided and abetted by the equally famous conductor Landon Ronald, were absolute sell-outs at each performance. The same season saw one of the biggest names in the world appearing at the Opera House; the great Charlie Chaplin was making his first appearance in the resort.

Another big name appeared in Blackpool on 24th September that year. At the Portland Trotting Track, situated off Whitegate Drive, the town was treated to a Wild West show, by none other than the dashing Buffalo Bill Cody and his Congress of Rough Riders of the World. The show, held under floodlights, comprised 800 people, 800 horses, and a variety of other animals and props, which had required three special trains to convey them to the resort, where the crowds were a sell out. What a star studded list of performers in one unbelievable season this was, and of course all the theatres in the resort played their part by featuring dozens of other top line artistes; no wonder then that Blackpool was so popular.

On the municipal front the biggest event was the granting of County Borough status to the town, and celebrations were held to mark the occasion. All school children were given a holiday and little mementoes, whilst parties were seen in abundance, as was the normal practice in those long gone days. This new corporate status was a fantastic achievement for a resort town that had only become an incorporated borough just over twenty six years previously, and had been little more than a village a generation or two earlier. The new status was almost equal to that of a city, and carried with it exactly the same powers. All this had been achieved by the same entrepreneurs and local worthies that had put the town now so firmly on the map in every sense of the word. Things were definitely looking up for the little town grown big overnight.

The new promenade celebrations of 1905

A well known phrase throughout show business goes something like this: "*You ain't seen nothing yet*". That saying could easily be applied to the celebrations taking place in Blackpool during the summer of 1905, due to the opening of the new promenade extensions that had just been completed.

The Promenade, which had begun in a rudimentary manner many generations ago, and which had subsequently been lengthened, strengthened and widened on many previous occasions had now undergone its biggest and most costly transformation to date.

From a point almost adjacent to North Pier, southwards to a point adjacent to the Victoria (South) Pier, the Promenade had been extended seawards by about one hundred feet, resulting in a new stone sea wall being constructed. Millions of tons of sand were used to infill the void that separated the old sea wall from the new, and a light railway dubbed the 'sands express' was constructed to supply the sand for the infill. This was then put into place by a vast army of workmen, the sand having being transported from the sand hills at South Shore. This undertaking, meticulously planned and overseen by Blackpool Borough Surveyor, James Brodie, was really a project of national importance. Not only did Blackpool reclaim many acres of land from the sea, but the new sea wall almost guaranteed that flooding would never return.

Blackpool's South Promenade before being renamed Central Promenade.

(Andrew Hazlehurst Collection)

Electrical Activity!

The town now witnessed several illuminations displays; lighting technology was coming on in leaps and bounds. Several tramcars had illuminated features and these machines aroused much interest and delight amongst the large crowds. Quite apart from the illuminated trams, the stalwarts of the town, such as the Tower and Winter Gardens, put on magnificent illuminated displays of their own. There was a new and significant development taking place by now, however, and that was the ongoing development of the Pleasure Beach at South Shore, by Messrs Bean and Outhwaite, where in 1904 they had opened their first electrically driven ride known as 'The Flying Machine'. This ride, incidentally, was invented by the Anglo-American Sir Hiram Maxim and still operates today.

Sir Hiram Maxim's Captive Flying Machine is under construction in 1904 at Blackpool's South Shore. A year later, this area would be first advertised as 'the Pleasure Beach'.
(Blackpool Pleasure Beach Archives)

Where and when the electricity first came from to service this ride is not quite clear, but Ted Lightbown's records show that Bean and Outhwaite were distancing themselves from the Machine's Sunday operations, due to the Council threatening to cut off the electricity supply. Sundays were taken very seriously back then.

Within a very short space of time, the Pleasure Beach grew large and busy. It was a very popular place where the Beans, and later the Thompsons (following the marriage of William Bean's daughter, Doris, to Leonard Thompson), followed the trends in fairground fashion. They imported many ideas from home and abroad – but primarily from the United States – from which country Alderman Bean had brought the idea of his amusement park. Electricity first appeared in a really big way at the Pleasure Beach in 1906, when the Blackpool Herald reported that the management there had applied for a supply of electricity to light arc lamps and 1,000 incandescent lamps in order to illuminate the new stalls being erected there. The Council had agreed to supply the electricity for this scheme. There are photographs in existence showing the poles carrying the overhead supply to the grounds.

The following is an extract taken from a full-page article that appeared in the Blackpool Herald on 26th July 1907 ('Electric lighting at the Pleasure Beach'); here you will see yet another precursor for the modern Illuminations as we know them today:

> "When dusk comes, a forest of great arc lamps of glorious brilliance burst into light and simultaneously ten thousand fairy lamps transform the Pleasure Beach into an enchanting fairyland. It is a splendid electrical display, and no one should miss seeing the lovely illumination down among the sand hills. All the great features, such as the Scenic Railway, the Canadian Water Chute, and the River Caves are a blaze of light, and the scene is one of surpassing beauty.
>
> All these beauteous electrical effects are produced and designed by Mr A. Mortimer, of Manchester and Blackpool, an engineer of great experience, and who is responsible for the lighting of the whole estate."

So those progressive business people who had so willingly jumped onto the electric lamp bandwagon were now dealing in *thousands* of lamps at one go, rather than the mere handful of a few years previously. Considering the general proliferation of electric lamps over the ensuing years it comes as no great surprise perhaps that Blackpool, always in the van in such matters, should actually go down the illuminated road, so to speak, becoming the first town in Britain to introduce the concept of an

The Water Chute at the Pleasure Beach in 1910.

(Nick Laister Collection)

annual light show. One point to bear in mind from these early years is the simple fact that not only did many of those who came to view the coloured lights not have electricity in the home; many even lacked gas lighting. Small wonder then that they thought the lights fantastic, as no doubt they did when visiting the Colosseum, Blackpool's first cinema, which was situated just behind the Promenade. This cinema was formed from a cast iron building previously erected on the Raikes Hall Gardens, where it housed the Niagara diorama.

On the electrical front, things continued to develop quickly, as the following extract from the 1906 Official Blackpool Guide shows:

"Artistic columns, bearing the latest arc lamps, are fixed, at short intervals, from end to end of the vast sea parades, and, as the brilliancy of the famous 'line of light' is added to by the illuminations of the piers and the huge places of entertainment the charms of the Blackpool front after nightfall quite correspond with the delights of the day. The whole of the principal thoroughfares – from North shore to South shore – are also brightly lighted with electric arcs and, as almost the whole of the window-featured tradesmen's establishments further contribute to the towns brightness, the setting of the sun merely serves as the signal for an artificial radiance such as is rarely met within the most advanced municipalities."

Blackpool's South Pier in 1907 (with a very ornate lamppost!).

(Andrew Hazlehurst Collection)

We can see from this report just what advances were being made not only in decorative lighting, but also in public lighting schemes for the main streets. We can

also see that the Blackpool publicity machine was working well, working on the basis of "if you have got it, then flaunt it". But what the official guide failed to mention was the sheer size of Blackpool's electrical output, which had grown in leaps and bounds since its inception during 1879. The output of the generating station had now reached some 4,450 kilowatts at full load, 1,750 of which were used to power the Corporation tramways.

The following several years saw many advances in Blackpool's continuing growth. New schools and churches were appearing in every district, whilst of course much construction work was being undertaken in both the domestic and commercial

sectors, where vast estates of housing were taking shape and many new hotels and boarding houses along with shops were also appearing.

During this period the Promenade was extended well past North Pier, whilst the Carnegie Library and the adjoining Grundy Art Gallery were opened at the junction of Queen Street and Maybell Avenue.

Throughout 1910, the output at Blackpool's electrical generating station, having undergone several improvements, rose sharply. It needed to do so, because not only were the trams demanding ever more output, but the number of private consumers had risen to 1,450. Many of these were hotels, but several were also private households. More streets were being lit by electricity; in fact there were now at least 272 arc lamps on the main highways, including the Promenade, whilst there were 772 incandescent lamps fixed to various arc lamp poles. The lamps along the tramway routes were placed on the same steel poles that carried the overhead power lines, whereas others were placed on ornate cast iron pillars. Both Blackpool Corporation Tramways and their rivals the Lytham and St Annes Tramway were supplied with power from the town's main generating station, as a small generator at Blundell Street had now been shut down for good.

Another Royal Occasion

Meanwhile King Edward VII had also died during this same year, so that by the following year, 1911, Blackpool saw further Royal celebrations due to the coronation of King George V and Queen Mary. As a result the town was 'en fete' once again.

Perhaps the high spot of the whole spectacle was the appearance of many illuminated features along the Promenade and, of course, on all the main theatres and public buildings, electric lighting was seen in abundance.

The town was also hit by a national rail strike in August. This caused quite a lot of aggravation for the thousands of trippers who were stuck in the resort due to lack of transport. The strike also caused trouble for those potential holidaymakers who had hoped to get to the seaside, but now were not able. Eventually the trains got back to normal, as did Blackpool, which thankfully avoided the violence seen in some other towns at the time.

Above left: **Gynn 1907 with separate tramways, before they combined.**
(Andrew Hazlehurst Collection)

Above right: **The Tower Ballroom in 1910.**
(Andrew Hazlehurst Collection)

A Titanic year

If 1911 had been a rather quiet year, at least judged by Blackpool's own standards, if not the nation's, then 1912 was to make up for it with a vengeance. 1912 was to be the year that the Illuminations changed from being an incidental part of Blackpool's attractions to a major annual event. In a year which saw the loss of the mighty Titanic, Blackpool conferred the freedom of the town onto to two of its most eminent citizens, namely Alderman John Bickerstaffe and Alderman James Fish, both members of the council.

On the entertainments scene there was a brass band concert in the Tower circus, whilst the great female star Miss Ellen Terry trod the boards in the theatre, and of course all the other theatres in the town featured many top line artistes playing to full houses. Meanwhile, down the coast a few miles, the racing season was in full swing at the Clifton Park Racecourse, situated at Squires Gate.

With regards to power supplies, reports that the Corporation Gasworks had turned in a profit of £14,700 for the year showed that that industry hadn't gone under to electricity. Despite the increased output from the recently extended electricity works, which were now going full swing, a lot of hard work was needed to keep up with the ever increasing demand, which would be added to by the imminent switch on of the lights at Princess Parade. Also at this time, the Admiralty was conducting experiments with ship to shore wireless telegraphy off Blackpool. This was taking place from the Tower top, along with an experiment in wireless communications that linked Blackpool Tower with the Eiffel Tower.

From the resort's point of view, however, the most important event was the opening of a new section of Promenade abutting the North Pier and

Bailey's Metropole Hotel. This Promenade was due to be opened by HRH the Princess Louise and her husband, the Duke of Argyll who, having arrived by train the evening of 30th April, were whisked to a welcoming banquet at the Imperial Hotel at North Shore. Here they were presented to the full council and a host of other worthies representing the business of the town.

The next day, the Princess and the Duke were conveyed by carriage to the appointed place where a ribbon was cut, and the huge crowd assembled, cheered in unison. The best was yet to come however as the area had been prepared with triumphal arches festooned in electric lamps, whilst the adjacent arc lamp standards were similarly treated, along with the ship's mast that had been erected on the green. The mast and the guy ropes leading from top to bottom had been festooned with a multitude of electric lamps, as had several other features nearby. In all, over ten thousand lamps lit the scene, and when the switch was thrown, another huge cheer came up from the equally huge crowd which comprised both locals and holidaymakers alike. All the prominent buildings in the town followed suit, each determined to outdo the other, whilst the Town Hall was absolutely resplendent with light, as was tramcar number 68, which was ablaze with the light of no less than 3,000 lamps!

This first annual illuminated event was the result of the vision of one man: Charles Furness, the Tramways and Electrical Engineer. Decorating the Promenade in this way had long been a goal of Furness, a goal he was to finally realise in 1912. It was also Furness who believed that the Council could create its own illuminations, rather than buy them in from outside suppliers. In short, it is without a doubt that Charles Furness was the man who created the modern-day Blackpool Illuminations.

One of the most amazing facts surrounding the event was that a motor car had been kept in wait for a specialist film crew which was to film the opening ceremony;

The assembled crowd welcomes Princess Louise and the Duke of Argyll on 1st May 1912.
(Andrew Hazlehurst Collection)

A lone figure surveys the 1912 Illuminations on Princess Parade.
(Andrew Hazlehurst Collection)

Before the war only the top of Blackpool Tower was illuminated. This picture shows the Princess Parade Gardens at night in 1912.
(Andrew Hazlehurst Collection)

the resulting film would then be whisked to Liverpool for developing in order that it might be shown in Blackpool the same evening. It was in fact delivered and screened at the Royal Pavilion situated on Rigby Road. Quite a remarkable feat for the times!

So well received were the Princess Parade lights – and the illuminated tram – that there were calls for an encore from several, including Alderman Tom Bickerstaffe. It is said he asked the electrical engineer, Charles Furness, his opinion as to whether or not the visitors might take to such displays on a permanent basis. The engineer answered in the affirmative and gave the Alderman an estimate of costs, which he in turn put to the Council. His words didn't fall on deaf ears, as the Council then decided to repeat the performance during September and October. These were the first 'regular' autumn Illuminations. The modern-day Blackpool Illuminations were well and truly born.

The 1913 Illuminations would again coincide with a Royal visit to the town, this time by the King and Queen. The new, bigger, lights scheme costing £2,000 was extended to cover an even larger area of Promenade. The Gazette News reported the scheme in great detail:

Princess Parade in 1912. Although on a smaller scale than today, the first Illuminations were no less awe-inspiring.

ILLUMINATIONS AT BLACKPOOL

"Twenty imposing Ionic columns festooned and picked out with multi-coloured lamps forming an unbroken chain of electric brilliants from Regent Square to Foxhall Square. From the 52ft mast in Queens Square are suspended six or seven festoons of lamps, making a huge canopy of fairy glow lights. Tram shelters at the Gynn, Warley Road, Derby Road, Talbot Square, Manchester Square and Victoria Pier

were lit up too, and there was a special display in Corporation Park near the Pleasure Beach. A triumphal arch was picked out and decorated with about 2,000 lamps. Eighteen toast rack trams, as well as other cars, were illuminated too. All told, over 60,000 lights were used in the display. They lasted from September 18th to October 18th, and covered three miles of seafront".

King George V and Queen Mary are introduced to Blackpool dignitaries during their 1913 visit.
(Andrew Hazlehurst Collection)

The main Illuminations were also supplemented by the now well established arc lamps, as well as many more features provided by private companies within the town. The whole scheme, having consumed 60,000 units of electricity, was so successful that the season was extended and the ensuing crowds so big that the railway companies and the resort had difficulty catering to their needs. It was now obvious to all that the visitor did indeed like the Illuminations and as a result henceforth they would be staged on an annual basis, starting next year in 1914. Of course at that particular time, few people could have imagined just what horrific events the future held. The coming season was therefore planned for in the usual way and all involved looked forward to a peaceful and prosperous season. Such thoughts were soon to be blown apart by a chain of events that would shake the very foundations of society.

A 'toastrack' tram travels along Abingdon Street, its lighting clearly visible.
(Terry Regan Collection)

5 Prelude to war

That fateful year of 1914 started in a similar fashion to previous years; the winter brought its usual crop of stormy weather and all those involved in the holiday industry spent the better part of the winter readying their premises for the summer season.

Winter gave way to spring and by the time Easter came around everything was going as normal. May was an eventful month, a month of major fires in fact. One might also have viewed his month as a precursor of things to come.

The first fire of note occurred on 12th May. The Fairyland amusement park was burnt to a cinder when an electrical fault in one of the carriages on the miniature railway that ran through the fairy grottoes sparked a huge blaze which soon spread to the rest of the building. Luckily the place was quickly evacuated and there were no injuries amongst the passengers and staff. The buildings next door contained a cinema, which was also in danger of destruction, and the only thing that enabled the fire crews to save the day was the use of an elevated platform belonging to the Tramways Department from which the firemen were able to direct jets of water onto the flames.

Another conflagration took place on 17th July. This time it was the Gasworks that went up in smoke and so fierce was the fire that it took three days to finally douse the flames.

The season was well and truly under way by this time and neither the odd spell of bad weather nor even a big fire or two wasn't going to spoil the fun for the day trippers. Unknown to them, of course, fate was conspiring to do just that.

A dim uproar

August 4th 1914 saw the outbreak of war. This threatened to put a stop to Blackpool's plans for the season, which was soon to see the Illuminations switched on once more. The first sign of trouble occurred when the Admiralty advised coastal authorities to dim their lights as the enemy might use them to their advantage. These words fell on deaf ears in Blackpool however as civic officials, aided and abetted by the big business bosses of the resort, decided to press ahead with the Illuminations.

This caused uproar and the local evening paper was seething in its condemnation of the lights that were shining merrily whilst British sailors were losing their lives at sea. The businessmen involved remained unconvinced as they felt that switching off the lights might cause wholesale bankruptcies. But the lights were finally extinguished on 19th October, not to be seen again until the 1920s.

This was not to be the case in the United States, however, where electrical development went on at an even faster pace, particularly in the development of lighting. There were many amusement parks in that country which utilised electricity to its maximum potential; these of course included the famous Coney Island, but also several other parks including Electric Park in Kansas City. Here the park, with its roller coasters and many other rides, was lit up by over one hundred thousand lamps, which shone without a blink throughout the duration of the War.

As with the majority of British towns, Blackpool suffered in many ways through this dreadful war; many local men were killed or wounded in action and as a result whole families suffered grief and hardship. Ironically though, the town experienced some of its best ever seasons! A majority of the largest hotels had been requisitioned by the War Department, being used for housing the troops and for training purposes. The Royal Army Medical Corps established its headquarters in the town and thousands of troops, along with the continuing trickle of day trippers, brought much needed revenue into the resort.

After the War there were held tribunals at which the hoteliers and tourist attractions were able to claim damages for loss of business; some made quite a packet. One of the most interesting claims for compensation came from the Winter Gardens Company, which claimed several thousand of pounds from the Admiralty which had requisitioned the Empress Ballroom on the basis of it being, reputedly, the largest room in the north of England.

This Ballroom was, however, not used for housing troops, but for the manufacture of airships! The roof of the ballroom was removed and an army of workers, mainly female, constructed the airships which were then filled with gas, floated skywards and moved across Morecambe Bay to the shipyards of Vickers at Barrow-in-Furness.

This pre WW1 photograph shows the Sunken Gardens on Blackpool's north cliffs by day.
(Andrew Hazlehurst Collection)

Imagine the scenes in the town centre as the airships were seen floating from within the Empress Ballroom; what a surreal spectacle this must have been.

By the second year of the War, Blackpool was enjoying something of a boom. A large military hospital was set up at Squires Gate, on the site of the recently bankrupt Clifton Park Racecourse. Huts and tents were erected here to accommodate a steady flow of wounded, and the old grandstand and racecourse buildings were also commandeered for this purpose. One rather macabre 'amusement' was provided in close proximity to the hospital, a mock-up of the 'Loos' trenches in Belgium. The public had to pay to go into the trenches, but the soldiers, if in uniform, could enter free. How many wounded men, having been evacuated from the Western front, took advantage of this offer is unknown, but surely the numbers must have been low!

The Tower continued with an Aquatic and Variety Circus, featuring Doodles and August the Clown, as well as the famous Lockhart's Elephants. Meanwhile, at the Princess Electric Theatre the main film showing was 'Emmy of Storks Nest', and at the Imperial Picture Palace we had 'The Fighting Hope'. In fact, all the theatres and cinemas did a roaring trade throughout the War. At the Grand Theatre, they were showing top line shows long before they ever reached the West End, including 'Chu Chin Chow', and the 'Maid of The Mountains'. Meanwhile, the Grundy Art Gallery staged a large exhibition of Canadian war photographs, which, strange to relate, was well supported.

Daily life in the resort carried on as normal in many ways. The improvements to the Promenade went on unabated, including the building of sunken gardens near the Gynn, even though there was a severe shortage of coal, savings being called for in its consumption. It was the same with gas and electricity, even though the Council's Street Lighting Committee had recently declared that the newly absorbed township of Bispham with Norbreck could expect its street lighting to be brought up to the same standards as the rest of Blackpool.

Blackpool's Princess Parade became home to a cenotaph, erected in memory of those lost in the war.

(Andrew Hazlehurst Collection)

The usual crop of 'Freemen' were created, day trippers came and went, their visits all the more poignant as the death toll mounted on the war front, no doubt a "live today and blow tomorrow" philosophy came into play, and who could really blame them for that?

As victory for the Allies looked more certain, the nation, now almost sapped of its strength and robbed of the cream of its young men, yearned for the day when peace would come, as it finally did on 11th November 1918. The reaction to the news was tremendous and joyful, as the following letter written to a local newspaper some years later by a Mr Halsall showed:

> "I was 14 and working at Pickerings grocers and butchers at the corner of Talbot Road, and Swainson Street. The Armistice was to be signed at 11am, and it was announced in the evening paper the night before, that a green flag would fly from the Tower top if it was signed, and a red flag if not. There was no radio then! Up went the green flag, and Blackpool went mad. That evening my pal and I went down to the promenade, and coming past North Pier towards us was a huge crowd of officers, all in hospital blue, from the Imperial Hydro, and the Metropole Hotel. In no time at all, Charlie and I were bang in the middle of the officers, being herded along, we knew not where. We went up a few marble steps, on up carpeted stairs, and there we were in the Dress Circle of the Palace. Top of the bill was shared between 'Mystery Raymond' and 'Dainty Doris Dormer'…the officers made such a racket throughout that she left the stage in tears, when Mystery Raymond came on stage and made a tear jerking patriotic speech, after which Daisy was judged to be so good they wouldn't let her leave the stage."

1919 saw the return of thousands of wounded troops and, as before, many thousands of these unfortunate men were sent to Blackpool for recuperation, resulting in the military hospitals in the resort being full to overflowing. The entertainment of this captive audience was of a high priority, and accordingly dances and shows were held on a regular basis for the men, some of whom took exception to the fact that there seemed to be bigger and better dances being held for the officers and their ladies. As a result there were several protest rallies in Talbot Square, and when the crowd heard a rumour that there was to be a big Victory Ball at the Tower – but that the ordinary soldier wouldn't be invited – there was a riot, which resulted in a mob rushing the Tower doors where they apparently threatened to throw the Mayor and the commanding officer into the sea. Eventually common sense prevailed, the men were let in, and the Mayor further placated them by the promise of more dances, to which all would be admitted free.

These are just two examples of how the sudden release of pent up emotion could affect people whose lives had been so blighted. It would be many years before the town got back to normal, and many years before Blackpool's Illuminations would shine again.

6 The Roaring Twenties

Wars are defining moments in history and so it was with the Great War, an event that had seen technology move forward in leaps and bounds, with an ever increasing use of electrical gadgetry by the military. Lighting had also improved immensely; arc lights and incandescent lamps being much more powerful than hitherto, and more streets were lit by electricity than ever before. Blackpool as usual was on the ball in this respect and very few towns actually spent a higher proportion of their rates on street lighting.

The re-introduction of the Illuminations was long overdue, but these were not normal times and such matters would have to wait. For a start, the coal mining industry had been badly hit during the war and the industry could barely keep pace with consumption at the power stations. The situation was worsened by the miners going on strike previously and the demand for coal at the power stations was not being met. Consequently it was several years before the lights would twinkle once again.

Blackpool didn't stand still though and various ideas to bring custom to the resort were proposed. Eventually it was decided to hold a Carnival such as they had recently held in Brighton. A spying trip headed by Alderman T. Bickerstaffe had visited Brighton and had reported back that they were very impressed and that Blackpool should follow suit.

A Carnival was quickly organised for the 1923 season, the team responsible for its implementation being those who ran the tramways and the Illuminations. A workshop was set up in the works yard, where floats, scenery, and various decorations were manufactured, the specialist work of creating dozens of gigantic papier mache heads being left to a group of skilled artists from Nice, who were drafted in for the purpose. This workshop would later provide the Illuminations with their first permanent home. The event opened at the new Open Air Baths to a fanfare of publicity, which also saw the opening of yet another new stretch of promenade.

Carnival week was a massive success and it has been estimated that perhaps two million people attended the event, with as many as three hundred thousand people a day taking part in the parades. Several hundred special trains brought in hundreds of thousands of trippers and with the rail traffic, the buses,

The Carnival in June 1923 was a major post-war attraction. A group in fancy dress pose in front of the Metropole Hotel, near North Pier. This was the site of the first Illuminations display.

All the stops were pulled out to make sure that the carnivals were a success. In 1923, crowds lined the route and a vast procession made its way along Blackpool's Promenade.

charabancs, private cars, motor cycles, and tens of thousands of cycles brought innumerable revellers to the event. Aircraft even got in on the act, as several hundreds of passengers were ferried to the resort from Manchester, whilst many locals also joined in the fun.

So successful was the Carnival, another was immediately planned for the following season and it now seemed Blackpool had replaced the lights with an even bigger money-spinner. Events were to prove those thoughts wrong.

Next season the crowds were equally immense, but it seems that the carnival had attracted many thugs and yobs, who were bent on causing disruption. Drunkenness and violence were rife.

The Blackpool public were outraged at these events, as were the authorities and as a result it was decided never to hold a Carnival again, but instead to consider reintroducing the Illuminations in time for the 1925 season. Pressure from the local chamber of trade played a big part in this decision. However, the new Illuminations were only seen on a limited scale, as electricity was still not freely available. Despite this the lights equipment having been stored in the tramways depot since 1914 was hurriedly checked out and made ready for use.

A relatively small display was implemented along the Promenade, stretching from the Manchester Hotel northwards to the Gynn Hotel. The lights were exceptionally well received, especially with the introduction of several naval searchlights, now surplus to war requirements. The trams carried more passengers than ever, the revenue they created being highly appreciated at the town hall. Mr F Field, the Tramways Manager, had designed a new illuminated tram in the form of a large Venetian Gondola, which apparently caused a sensation amongst the crowds. At this point in time it is very clear that Blackpool's prosperity owed much to the Tramways Department.

'The Frog Who Would a Wooing Go' tableau in 1928. Early tableaux consisted of painted plywood scenes illuminated by lamps. Note the sandbags to help balance the tableau against the strong winds blowing from the Irish Sea.

A Bitter Sweet Jubilee

The following year, 1926, was actually Blackpool's 50th anniversary of becoming an incorporated borough, a Jubilee year that had long been awaited and for which big plans had been made. Almost all in the town looked forward to a joyful year, and a prosperous season to boot. The fates being what they are, however, had other plans. The year started with a tremendous storm that not only piled sand several feet high along the Promenade and other exposed places, but also caused tens of thousands of pounds worth of damage to properties in the resort.

By the time the spring arrived Blackpool had dusted itself down and things were getting back to something approaching normal. The biggest and best lights display ever was being planned for the autumn season and many well known names in theatre had been booked in advance. Much construction work was underway in the town; shops and hotels were either being built or were being modernised, several new cinemas were being introduced, and there was a string of private housing schemes under way.

The Council was not being left behind during this building boom though, for it was actively implementing a large programme of council house development in various quarters of the Borough, although oddly, many of these homes were not wired for electricity! The Council was extremely busy improving the Promenade at South Shore yet again and had also employed the services of the famous architect TH Mawson. This man had been called in to design a huge public park, which when it was eventually completed by a vast army of skilled tradesmen and labourers – brought in from as far afield as Belfast and Glasgow – was to be called Stanley Park, in honour of Lord Stanley. This scheme had the benefit of giving some employment, if not much money, to many of those poor people who had been thrown out of work during the recent slump. Their labours bequeathed the town with a fantastic legacy for all to enjoy.

Big celebrations were held in the Town Hall in order to celebrate the Jubilee; many important guests from all walks of life were invited. In conjunction with this activity, the town saw the creation of several new Freemen, including Sir Lindsay Parkinson, the Mayor, Alderman T. Bickerstaffe, along with the well known theatrical figure Alderman WH Broadhead, whilst a previous Freeman, John Bickerstaffe, was created a knight of the realm.

Away from such activities, the holiday season opened in its usual way, but by the time the traditional wakes weeks came around there was a distinct trend towards a quiet season, this no doubt due to the ever increasing industrial trouble afflicting the country. However, despite the misgivings, the Lights were switched on as planned on 24th September, for the first time extending all the way from South Shore to the Gynn. But by now a general strike was underway and, as a result of which, the Government ordered Blackpool to switch the lights off again. At first the Council defied the Government; that is, until the minister involved threatened to commandeer Blackpool's Electricity Works. The Council was given special permission to stage the lights, but for one night only on 2nd October, due to the opening of the new promenade and Stanley Park by Lord Derby.

Opened in 1923, the Open Air Baths at South Shore soon became a popular attraction.
(Andrew Hazlehurst Collection)

**The South Shore Baths
in 1928.**

All this was a great shame as the public saw precious little of what were the "biggest and best" Illuminations, with their 250,000 light bulbs and yet another specially illuminated tram, this time shaped like a lifeboat and named 'Jubilee'. Other features included a display with a Venetian flavour at the Open Air Baths, where several wooden rowing boats were disguised as gondolas, and scenery was introduced that mimicked the canals of that famous city, the whole scene vividly floodlit. The Electricity Department laid on a special cheap electrical supply to Blackpool businesses and tourist attractions, to encourage the illumination of buildings. As further encouragement, an annual competition was launched to find the best private illuminated display.

It wasn't only the day tripper who was disappointed, however, as by now the lights had become something of a national institution. Not only did such newspapers as the Daily Telegraph, and even The Times, express their disappointment at the cancellation, but a large electrical manufacturing company, The Imperial Lighting Company of London, also expressed their dismay, having been heavily involved in the development of new lighting displays specially created for the Jubilee. The strike had delivered a fatal blow to Blackpool's season and many traders were faced with bankruptcy. It was back to the drawing board and hopefully a better year next time around.

A buzz of activity

No one knew it at the time of course, but 1927 was to be yet another watershed year, a year that saw many strange and exciting events, as well as setbacks. The year kicked off once again in the by now time honoured fashion. The winter season that followed the short lived Christmas and New Year celebrations, with its pantomimes and children's balls (often referred to by locals as 'the kipper season') was now over, the boarding houses and 'joints' on the Golden Mile were all prepared for action and things were slowly beginning to settle down after the industrial unrest.

By the spring there was a buzz in the air, and the local builders were once again busy. Many private homes were under construction, and the local authority were busy building new roads and public recreation grounds, whilst at Talbot Square they were implementing a scheme of road widening to accommodate the increase in road traffic there. The Miners Convalescent Home had just been completed and formally opened on the Queens Promenade at Bispham. It was built by Sir Lindsay Parkinson and Co, as was the Queens Brewery on Talbot Road and the brand new girls secondary school on Beech Avenue adjacent to Stanley Park. In the Park itself there was a ceremony held in which Sir John Bickerstaffe cut the ribbon at the huge Cocker memorial clock tower, built to honour Blackpool's first and longest serving Mayor, a man of great vision, who foresaw the town's rise to fame.

Many top artistes and shows were due to be staged in the town. The Grand Theatre staged 'No No Nanette', and the Palace featured Jack Hylton and his Band. At the North Pier there was 'On with the Show' with Jan Ralfini and his Band, along with the perennial Fred Walmesley. Central Pier had the Wylie Tate Super Pierotts, whereas the Victoria (or South) Pier starred Catlins Royal Pierrots. The Pleasure Beach advertised such items as The Indian Temple Of Mystery, the House Of Nonsense, the Big Dipper, the Velvet Coaster and 'Gorgeous Electrical Illuminations'. At the Opera House, Margaret Bannerman appeared in 'The Zoo', whilst at the Tower and the Winter Gardens there were midget shows (how times have changed for the better!) Not to be left out, the many cinemas were showing top rank films. At the Tivoli we had 'Men of the Night', at the Hippodrome 'Loves Blindness' and at the Princess, Dorothy Gish starred in 'London'.

Of Course the Illuminations were due to be the "biggest and best" once again. Consumption of electricity was surging once more after the serious coal shortages in the recent past, as shown by the article in the Evening Gazette headed 'An Electric Year', where councillor Fred Boothroyd confidently expressed his views that more than 2,000 extra customers would enjoy electricity in their homes, now supplied from the giant generating works in Preston. Ironically, it was investment in electricity generating in Preston that allowed the Blackpool Illuminations to expand; the completion of new transmission lines from the massive new Penwortham Power

**Blackpool's North Pier –
'On with the Show' 1928.**

Station made the bigger 1927 Illuminations possible. The small Blackpool generating station at West Caroline Street was no longer able to cope with demand and was only used as a booster station. In only a few short years, Preston would be supplying 90% of Blackpool's electricity.

Of interest, a report in the Gazette and Herald of 28th June showed that there had been a big increase in the consumption of electricity.

> "The total output at the Blackpool Works was 1,932,650 units, an increase of nearly half a million units on last year; during the past two months 282 new consumers were connected. During the five weeks ending June 16th, Blackpool Trams carried 3,920,560 passengers, an increase of 358,826 on last year; from April 1st to the above date the passengers numbered nearly eight million, an increase of almost a million, the receipts being £57,965, an increase of £6,653. The average receipts per tramcar mile were 1/10d, whilst the buses generated only 11d, exactly half! At Whitsuntide the trams carried 1,869,568 passengers, an increase over the previous year of 346,776."

From the above figures it can be seen just how important the trams were to the local economy and it can also be seen just how vital trams were during the Illuminations periods, as the numbers of passengers carried during the lights far exceeded any other comparable part of the season.

The Prince of Wales visited the town on 28th June in order to open the Miners Convalescent Home. The next day the town experienced a singular event that quite literally put all others in the shade. This was the long awaited total eclipse of the sun, a phenomenon so rare as to cause great excitement throughout the resort, where many entertainments had been planned in order to take advantage of this wonderful event. Some primitive peoples might take such happenings as an omen, whereas in Blackpool it was seen as a money spinner. Newspapers carried advice on how to safely view the eclipse and also carried reams of adverts for many amusement centres and the like within the town, all of which extolled the virtues of their establishment as an advantageous point from which to view the sky. At the Tower there were plans to hold a dinner dance followed by an ascent in order to gain the best view of the eclipse, whilst the Winter Gardens were holding an eclipse dance, as were many of the larger hotels in town. At Squires Gate, several aircraft companies actually planned flights into the darkened sky, and as they said, you won't get a better view than from the air. Over one hundred thousand eager observers lined the Promenade, straining their necks and hoping for the best view of all.

After the excitement caused by the eclipse, the season went its merry way. The crowds arrived and departed as usual, and there was nothing to suggest that impending disaster was nigh. The autumn Illuminations were better than ever, several new features appeared, including giant butterflies which were strung over the carriageway along the Central Promenade. There was also an avenue of similar lights depicting young ladies dressed as 'Flappers'. It had also been decided that the lights would stay on until midnight for the very first time, this being due to the expected chaos at the railway stations, as had happened the previous year when the stations could not cope with the sudden rush of trippers wanting to get the train home. The expected crowds came and adored the show and many thousands of pounds found their way into the local economy. It seemed, at last, all was going well with the Blackpool money making machine. Until, that is, a sudden deterioration in the weather occurred.

Although bad weather is common at lights time, this year was different as the storm struck on 28th October 1927, smashing into the coastline from Fleetwood

Mickey Mouse tableau 1928.

down to Lytham. The sand dunes at St Annes and Squires Gate were absolutely inundated, as a result of which the trams couldn't operate in the area, and at one point the electricity failed completely. Further up the coast at South Shore, the new promenade was ripped to pieces as if an earthquake had struck. The Open Air Baths were badly hit, as was the Pleasure Beach and the surrounding area, and any Illuminations equipment still in situ was torn apart. At the Central Beach and the Golden Mile a lot of damage was inflicted, the floods reaching inland for hundreds of yards. Further north still, the North Pier was badly damaged, and Cocker Square was also flooded, while at Bispham the cliffs were pulverised and a tram was overturned by the wind near to St Stephens Avenue.

The further north one went then the greater the damage. Cleveleys and Thornton Gate were devastated by the force of the wind and floods, but it was at Fleetwood that the bulk of the damage occurred. This damage was estimated at the time to have cost a quarter of a million pounds (many millions today!), but that was not the worst part. At least six people had been drowned and many more had been marooned, several of whom had to be rescued by boats brought from Stanley Park lake. Meanwhile, hundreds of sheep and cattle also perished and many parts of the town suffered severe flood damage, some of which is evident even today.

Amazingly, despite the chaos, the tramways announced that they had beaten all records and carried almost six million fare paying passengers and also used an enormous amount of electricity in doing so, during the 31 days the lights were on. Quite a year by anyone's standard!

Down with the wheel!

In a rather curious way, Blackpool had reached a stage in its history, where people were beginning to expect great and unusual things to occur during the course of each coming year. In effect the town had become the star, as opposed to being just a venue for the stars of stage and screen. 1928 was such a year, but of course even the local Gypsies, armed as they were with crystal balls and the benefit of palmistry, couldn't really know what lay ahead for the town, which had become used to life on a roller coaster, with so many ups and downs. Naturally though, the local entertainment houses, as so many times before, had their plans, whilst as usual there was much activity in the local community, private, commercial and municipal.

For instance, the only obstacle that had stood in the way of a takeover of the Winter Gardens by its giant rival, the Blackpool Tower Company, came in the shape of the Managing Director of the Gardens, John Richard Huddlestone. The Tower Company had been hoping for years that an opportunity to take over the Gardens would present itself, and now it did, due to the fact that Huddlestone had died. So

Left: **A post-war view of Blackpool's Princess Parade. In 1920 only street lighting could be seen on the Promenade. It would be another five years before the Illuminations returned.**

Below: **Nursery rhymes have played a central part in many tableaux over the years. In the 1928 tableau, 'Hi Diddle Diddle', we see the dish running away with the spoon.**

well liked and respected was this former Rochdale lad, that over 50,000 mourners lined the streets when his funeral cortege passed by. Without a doubt he was one of the giants on the local scene and one of only a handful who had made the town so famous. In the following February it was proposed that a merger of the two companies should take place and without further ado the empire was formed. In the past the Tower Company had few, if any, rivals in the town; now they were almost completely dominant.

Another happening in the world of theatre occurred when Bannisters Bazaar, situated on the site of the old Borough Theatre, near Central station, was sold, only to become yet another theatre. Feldman's Theatre, as it became known, traded for several decades, until it too was sold, becoming transformed into the Queens Theatre. In time this also disappeared when the site was redeveloped for shops.

More unwelcome change came when the decision was taken to dismantle the Big Wheel at the Winter Gardens. The Wheel had been losing money for some time now and was also considered old fashioned and cumbersome, so down it came. The site was soon redeveloped as the Olympia amusement complex, thus depriving Blackpool of one of its most recognisable

landmarks. As previously mentioned, the resort was in a constant state of flux; there was no reason that such conditions shouldn't apply during 1928.

The autumn Illuminations were, however, staged exactly as planned, even though financial constraints were placed on the organisers who had managed to introduce several new features to the display, including floodlighting and multi-coloured festoons of lamps at the North Shore sunken gardens. To break up the monotony of Blackpool's long, straight Promenade between Pleasure Beach and Talbot Square, decorative arches had been constructed at Manchester Square and Pleasure Beach. Ideally, more of these would have been constructed, but they were prohibitively expensive. The solution: lighting features suspended between two lattice pylons; this created the illusion of a decorative arch, but was only a fraction of the cost.

One particularly impressive feature in this year was a display of huge butterflies, constructed on wire frames; girls reclining in hammocks appeared to float in the air.

The lights had once again saved the day as hundreds of thousands of day trippers poured in to view them. This influx allowed the tramways to carry so many passengers, that over £42,000 was raised in fares. What a huge debt Blackpool owed to its pioneers of electricity!

Above and right: **Huge butterflies on wire frames and girls in hammocks, both features of the 1928 display, looked like they were just hanging in the air.**

Boom in the doom and gloom

As the Twenties drew to a close, more and more people were on short time working, or out of work altogether, whilst others had to suffer pay cuts. All in all the situation was looking grim both at home and abroad. Although, as one might have expected, the tourist industry put on a brave face and announced plans for the season, more in hope than expectation that the trippers would return en masse.

The usual crop of big names visited the town, including the Prime Minister, Stanley Baldwin, whilst a Greek prince dropped in to say "hello" at the Mayors parlour, both visits duly recorded in the Evening Gazette, Blackpool's brand new evening newspaper. Meanwhile, the cinemas were advertising top flight 'talkies'.

On the Promenade, meanwhile, the stalls and booths along the Golden Mile were geared up for business. The usual crop of freak shows were ready for action, as was a Dutchman by the name of Sacco; this man was aiming to break the world's record for fasting whilst watched by thousands of enthralled visitors. His fast lasted from mid July until mid September, but unfortunately he died several weeks later.

At about the same time the Tussauds Waxworks were opened, and this new venture, situated as it was on the Golden Mile almost next door to Fairyland, was an instant success, as was the Kings Cup Round Britain Air Race, Blackpool being chosen as a halting place for the aircraft.

Once again the resort, despite all the predictions of doom and gloom, was booming; the builders were engaged in every sphere of construction. New schools were opened on behalf of the Council, and a new municipal airport was opened at Stanley Park. New highways were created, causing the inevitable housing estates that followed in their wake. Buildings all over the town were given their usual lick of paint, and business was better than many had dared hope for.

The railway companies, having learned the lessons of previous years, made sure that they had enough trains available with which to carry home the tens of thousands of trippers who were certain to converge on the two stations in order to catch the

To break up the monotonous festoon, illuminated arches were built at certain points along the Promenade. The Manchester Hotel can be seen on the left of this 1928 view.

train home. It was hoped that the crowds would get even bigger during the Illuminations, as for the first time ever all three piers had agreed to be illuminated from end to end. This decision meant that not only would there be well in excess of 100,000 coloured lamps along the Promenade, but with the displays at such venues as the Tower, the Winter Gardens and the Pleasure Beach, there may have been a quarter of a million lamps.

New features were introduced at the Open Air Baths, where an illuminated yacht floated on the water, whilst several large illuminated arches spanned the roadway. At the Town Hall, features included flashing signs and illuminated stars, while on the Promenade there were several 'kaleidoscopic' features in conjunction with 'crystal' devices containing flashing lights. At Manchester Square a scaled down illuminated windmill was constructed, complete with revolving sails, powered by some defunct machinery from the Pleasure Beach.

There was also a trial run with an illuminated aeroplane. The aircraft, having been dotted with about one hundred white lights, was meant to fly over and along the Promenade. However there seems to be no record of the event 'taking off', so to speak, as newspaper reports fail to mention it. Perhaps it was deemed too risky, as was another experiment in seaborne lighting displays: it seems that several floating tableaux were erected on pontoons just offshore, a good idea at the time, but not so

A girl admires this larger-than-life peacock feature in 1928.

good when the sea got choppy; the tableaux sank, and so did the idea, never to surface again!

Added to all of the above was that by now the competition to judge the best private lights display was also well underway. Many private hotels and other establishments entered, each hoping to win the prize donated by the Council. No wonder that Freddie Field, the Transport Manager, working under the auspices of Charles Furness, Tramways Manager and Electrical Engineer, was so enthusiastic at the press briefing prior to switch-on.

From the moment the lights were switched on, they were a great success. The railway companies between them carried more passengers into the resort than ever before. The crowds, however, had not only arrived by train, but many, many thousands had arrived by coach, car, bus and cycle. As a result the roads were absolutely full and chaos reigned. The hotels had had a 'burster', cafes and shops reported good profits, the traders along the Promenade were smiling, and by the close of business during those epic 31 nights of the lights, the tramways had smashed all records, having carried the grand total of 6,275,715 passengers, thus generating at least another £47,000 for the town's coffers.

All in all the season had been a success, although of course there was the inevitable

Blackpool's Talbot Square in 1928.

setback or two, but usually this was due to the weather, rather than problems in the industrial and financial world. In fact, the season had gone much better than at first feared, proving once again the immense pulling power of Blackpool. The question being asked now though was: could it last? And what did the future hold for the resort? The answers to these questions would soon be apparent to all, as the decade drew to a close and the news of the Wall Street Crash made its impact upon the world.

7 Clouds on the horizon

On 29th October 1929, there was financial meltdown in the US Stock Market, following a massive drop in iron and steel production. This heralded a massive depression that would affect the whole world.

Despite the global gloom Blackpool planned, as usual, for the summer season and hoped for a good one. Not being heavily industrialised, the impact of the Wall Street Crash was not expected to be felt quite as sharply as it was in other locations. It was, however, only to be expected that there would be some long term impact if the forecasts of financial disaster proved true.

As it turned out there was success in Blackpool that awful year. Blackpool Football Club was promoted to Division One for the first time and a crowd estimated at 30,000 packed Talbot Square to greet the players, led by the great Jimmy Hampson. On the theatre circuit the Opera House and The Grand were featuring top line West End plays, and amongst the star names to visit the town was Noel Coward, JB Priestly, and the writer Edgar Wallace, who stayed in his usual suite at the Metropole Hotel. On the North Pier, as usual, there was Lawrence Wright's 'On with the Show' and at the Palace of Varieties one of the leading turns was Harry Lauder. All in all then, it seems the year was not quite so bad as first feared, especially when the remarks of Alderman T. G. Lumb, Chairman of the Transport and Electricity Committee, are taken into account, when he described the Illuminations as a "Golden Stream Of Light". He went on to state that the number of passengers carried by tramcars during the lights' 31 days amounted to 6,400,000, bringing a total revenue of £47,500. The trams incidentally carried the majority of passengers in the town, and it would be many years before the buses were able to pay their way and eventually challenge the dominance of the tram, but that's another story!

Trams save the day

1930 got off to the kind of start one might normally expect in a Blackpool year. Winter gave way to a cold and blustery spring. The early season weather interfered with the routine maintenance of properties along the Promenade and adjoining districts, also at times interfering with the huge project of reconstruction taking place at the North Shore cliffs, where a giant lift was being installed. But by the start of the season

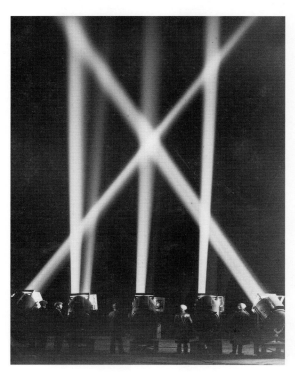

The searchlights on the Golden Mile in 1937 all had to be operated manually. These were later requisitioned for the war effort, being utilised at the industrial ports.

proper, everything was in place and the town was raring to go, the only question being, of course, would the holidaymakers and the day trippers arrive in numbers as before?

As the summer unfolded the weather remained unsettled, but nevertheless the day trippers began to arrive, their numbers perhaps depleted a little, but they were arriving as hoped for, seemingly hell-bent on enjoying themselves, come what may. And enjoy themselves they did, as all the local tourist traps such as the piers, the Golden Mile, the Tower and the grand panoply pulled out all the stops. This season saw a big increase in the numbers of visitors to Stanley Park, which by now had been completed, and would soon house the now defunct lifeboat, the Samuel Fletcher, on the lake, plying for hire as a pleasure craft.

A young girl is bemused by the four legs on each of the ugly sisters, in 1931. The latticework frame gives strength to a tableau, but still allows the winds to blow though.

By the end of the summer season proper, it was evident that trade was down somewhat, and again as in the recent past, traders and hoteliers were hoping that the lights would bail them out once again. They needn't have worried, for the lights, which were better than ever, did the trick once again. New features had been introduced the previous season that had seen animated lights displays depicting characters from fairy stories. These displays were now introduced on a bigger scale. On the cliff tops at Bispham, the first illuminated tableaux were introduced. Several more ex-naval searchlights were brought into play, and even the Cenotaph was floodlit for the very first time. All in all, considering the financial woes being suffered by the world at large, Blackpool had worked the oracle and on a shoestring budget had produced a stunning display, which had the effect of placating the trippers who hailed mainly from the troubled industrial towns. Indeed, Blackpool was in effect a kind of social safety valve, this syndrome would become even more apparent in the not too distant future as industrial relations became extremely fraught.

On a brighter note, however, it must be noted that yet again the tramways had broken all existing records; this time they had carried 6,617,167, passengers, contributing the handsome sum of well over £50,000 to the Borough's finances.

Blackpool soldiers on

As the decade lengthened, the financial trouble blighting the world began to take a bigger hold. In many countries, including Britain and America, there was civil unrest with rioting and food shortages in places. On the continent there were visible signs of violent times ahead, due to the rise of Communism and the Fascists.

More and more workers were unemployed, many more on short time, and money was in very short supply. These conditions applied even to Blackpool, where amongst the poorest there was real deprivation, and had it not been for such charities as the Foxton Dispensary, and the Chief Constables Clothing Fund, then the situation may well have been even worse. However, all was not bad news; indeed, as the decade wore on, Blackpool became even busier than usual (perhaps more evidence of the "live for today" syndrome?). The town saw many new public buildings rise, such as the Talbot Road Bus Station, and the long lamented Derby Baths at North Shore. Several huge department stores were constructed, along with new and improved highways, and scores of housing estates, both municipal and private. One important sign of the times was the big increase in the number of pawn-shops, second hand shops, and salerooms in the borough.

The average British town during the thirties was struggling for survival, and although it is true to say that there were pockets of real poverty and high unemployment in Blackpool at the time, it is equally true to state that Blackpool on the whole seemed to prosper. In the eyes of some this decade was regarded as its heyday, although of course such views are highly subjective.

The lights glow brightly in the gloom

Topping the bill at the Opera House in 1931 was Gracie Fields. This lass played to packed houses wherever she appeared, and Blackpool was no exception. In fact, her welcome was tremendous every time she appeared in the resort, whether just to sing or, indeed, to make movies. Gracie was only one of a whole host of stars appearing, some of whom were very big, including the American bass singer Paul Robeson.

The Winter Gardens saw the completion of the Galleon Bar and the Spanish Hall, but sadly, Fairyland, at Central Beach, was destroyed yet again by fire. The death of Claude 'Ohmy', the circus performer and proprietor, was announced, whilst at Stanley Park, the Prime Minister Ramsay Macdonald opened the town's new municipal airport (on the spot now occupied by the zoo). One of the highlights of this event was a lecture on aviation given by the famous woman pilot Amy Johnson, who had recently flown to Australia. Amy often came to stay in Blackpool in fact, from where, during a flight to the South of England, she disappeared without trace.

At this point in time live theatre was beginning to struggle in the resort. As in the rest of the country, money was in short supply and as a result the theatres couldn't afford to pay wages from the proceeds of half empty houses. This in turn forced many theatres to show films during the winter, and indeed right up until Whitsuntide in some cases, only Feldman's having an early season variety show. This move did, though, benefit the local people who were able to see first run movies at a knock-down price. Films included 'Charlie Chan Carries On' at the Grand. Edward G Robinson appeared in 'Little Caesar' at the Hippodrome, whilst at the Tivoli we were treated to 'The Lion and the Lamb'.

Blackpool was a town of paradoxes; whilst a number of showplaces were now starting to struggle, the Central Pier Company announced a 12% dividend, a big return even by their own standards. It appears also that the lights had done their job once again, despite cut backs, as the following report taken from the 21 September 1931 edition of the Coventry Guardian shows;

> "Blackpool, Sunday. As early as six o'clock yesterday morning the first special trains arrived at Blackpool bringing thousands of visitors to see the illuminations which opened their month's season last night. It was nearly three o'clock this morning before the last of the day trippers left. And at that hour a merry train load left the Central Station for Rowley Regis, near Worcester…one of the most effective novelties is the display of the big searchlights at the end of the three piers. Their beams cross each other constantly and weave patterns on the waves. The four mile promenade is a mass of colour. At the Open Air Bath, brilliant gondolas skim the water and fairy tales are told in changing lights. A glittering 'waterfall' decorates the bandstand."

One of the most memorable of the early tableaux was Cinderella. This tableau told the famous fairytale in light, with illuminated cut-out shapes of characters mounted

'You shall go to the ball.' A scene from the Cinderella tableau of 1931.

on a large wooden frame and supported with scaffolding poles. This tableau is all the more important as it was an early example of the use of a sequence controller, where groups of lights could be switched on separately from other parts of the display to create the illusion of animation. This animation allowed the ugly sisters to walk, the fairy to wave her wand and the prince to give Cinderella her missing slipper.

High Society

Late in the summer of 1932 a huge air pageant was held at the Airport, a very noisy event that attracted huge crowds. Shortly after this event, a further omen of bad times appeared in the form of the 'Graf Zeppelin', the German airship, which overflew the town, which now, rather oddly, possessed two airports. To complete this rather unusual demonstration of Blackpool's prowess in the flying arena, we had a visit from Captain Neville Stack, who had just flown an aircraft named 'Blackpool', all the way from India.

This particular year had started off on a very low note when, on 13th January, the biggest fire in the history of the resort took place at RHO Hills department store on Bank Hey Street. Damage was severe, resulting in the total destruction of the store, with several adjoining properties also badly damaged. The damage ran into several millions of pounds (at today's rates), whilst also injuring several firemen, who had battled valiantly to quell the blaze.

Amongst the many big names to appear in the resort that season were Stan Laurel and Oliver Hardy. The town went mad when they appeared to rapturous applause. The season was busy as usual, but the impact of the financial crisis was beginning to have an effect and many traders were forced to cut prices, whilst the big amusement centres were now giving large discounts on admission charges. Eventually the Illuminations season saved the day, but it was obvious that from now on Blackpool was going to have to become even thriftier if it was to succeed in the coming years.

The year that had started so badly now drew to an equally bad close when there was a large demonstration outside the Town Hall by unemployed workers. By the time 1933 came around it was obvious that Blackpool was going to be affected by the world situation after all.

Animation on the clifftops

1933 came in with a big freeze; ice and snow were everywhere, and this time Blackpool didn't escape. The ice on Stanley Park Lake was reported to be six inches thick, and due to this the locals who were brave enough to venture out onto the surface were treated to an exhilarating excursion at no cost.

It was a long and bitter winter though with many on the dole in the town, but eventually the world spun around and spring arrived to the relief of all. The town put on its summer attire, and sat back waiting for the trippers to arrive.

At the Imperial Hydro there was a conference held by the Municipal Tramway and Transport Association. This conference, their 32nd, was being held in Blackpool as recognition of the town's pioneering work in the introduction of electricity. In the chair being Charles Furness, Blackpool's Chief Electrical Engineer, and Consultant of Transport. As one might expect, Mr Furness extolled the virtues of trams and he educated the audience with the problems Blackpool had faced, and continued to face in staging the annual autumn Illuminations. The problems he made reference to were in relation to the weather, and the salt laden atmosphere along the Promenade, all of which had forced his department to experiment with new developments, many of which were now accepted as standard throughout the industry.

At this point it is worth noting a startling paradox, a paradox that applied equally to the whole of Britain. There is absolutely no doubt that the country as a whole was now struggling financially and yet consumerism appeared to be growing. The national and local newspapers were full of adverts for all things electrical; washing machines were readily available, as were wireless sets and gramophones. Vacuum cleaners galore were seen in the ads, as too were such luxuries as electric shavers and refrigerators. The paradox of course was the simple fact that the vast majority of the population couldn't afford such things and, furthermore, a percentage of their homes didn't even possess an electricity supply, so even if by chance they did manage to purchase such articles, some couldn't possibly use them.

Blackpool fitted well into such a paradox, for the more the country struggled, the more determined were the potential holidaymakers to visit the resort. One of many schemes introduced in order to entice the hard pressed public to the town was 'Guest Week'. This scheme involved the visitor claiming vouchers from the Publicity Department in order to get discounts off accommodation, goods and services, and in the early season it proved quite a success.

On the entertainment front, big names included George Formby at the Palace Varieties; he of course became such a regular visitor to the resort that he eventually bought a home just outside the town. At the Tower there was Bertini and his Orchestra, and that wonderful Wurlitzer player, Blackpool's own Reginald Dixon. Also at the same venue there was a once only appearance of the world famous Duke Ellington and his Jazz Band.

North Pier continued with its annual standby 'On with the Show' and at the Opera House we saw Leonard Laurence and Company starring in a show entitled 'Pleasure Cruise'. Meanwhile, at Squires

A tram passes Blackpool's North Pier in the early 1930s. 'On with the Show' was still packing in the crowds.

Above: **Christmas Scene 1933.**

Left: **It was a difficult job to lift and hold the tableaux in place whilst they were fitted to the poles. It also required a lot of men. The 'Prehistoric Blackpool' tableau is seen here in 1938.**

Gate, a second Greyhound racing track opened in conjunction with Sylvester's Modern Circus, featuring many elephants and all the usual circus entertainments.

The many cinemas were also showing the latest features, including 'If I had a Million' at the Hippodrome, a very apt title considering the present financial situation at large.

As autumn approached, plans for the lights were revealed. A huge publicity poster showed a sinuous young female wearing a vivid flame coloured costume, against a dark blue sky background, upon which searchlights wove an intricate pattern.

The Lights display had now been extended to cover almost five and three quarter miles of the Promenade, with several new features introduced, including many more animated tableaux along the cliff tops, arches galore and cartoon characters. All was not well, though, for even though the expected crowds did arrive, and though the roads were absolutely choc-a-bloc with motor vehicles, it emerged that the Lights were not as cost effective as many had believed. It was alleged that in fact they were being heavily subsidised by the Transport Department. Of course, those in charge of the Lights saw the matter from another viewpoint, however, as no doubt they argued that without the Lights then the buses and trams wouldn't carry half so many passengers, and probably this was true.

Bracing exhilaration!

The winter of 1934 saw even more people thrown out of work than before, the situation in America having become desperate. Blackpool, where wintertime unemployment was high, but where true industrialisation was low, was spared the full impact of the world situation; nevertheless the town was increasingly feeling the pinch, and the traders in the town were viewing the coming of each season with more than a little trepidation. Had it not been for the fact that Blackpool's workforce tended to be very loyal, and that the Council was being run by men of the highest

calibre, then the big businesses in the resort might have had even more to worry about. As it was, the workers in the town accepted wages that were often below the national average, working on the old adage of half a loaf being better than none, and the Council, for its part, was doing a magnificent job holding the town together by investing heavily in capital spending programmes, thus instilling a sense of optimism in the future.

Lord Derby visited the town in order to lay the foundation stone of the new Technical College in Palatine Road, on the site of a disused brickworks. Several council housing estates were initiated, with further extensions to some already in existence. But easily the biggest undertaking of the year on behalf of the Council was the massive extension of the town's boundaries that occurred during the amalgamation of almost the whole of Marton, save for that part abutting Lytham, and

also the annexing of parts of Hardhorn-With-Newton, Carleton, and Staining. So now we had the situation whereby the little upstart of a hamlet, Le Poole, had grown beyond its wildest dreams.

As the summer season passed quickly in its time honoured way, one of the biggest events was the massive fire at the Pleasure Beach, resulting in the total destruction of the Electric Theatre and the popular miniature railway. It was apparent that the lights would now be even more vital to the economy of the town, and with that in mind, whatever capital could be spared was thrown into the pot, resulting in a stunning show being created on the proverbial shoestring. The lights were better than ever, the trams carried more passengers than ever, the roads were jammed, and the railways could barely cope. Due to the volume of traffic, the entire Promenade was designated a one-way street at weekends (the north-south arrangement introduced in 1934 was reversed in 1938 and would then last until the end of the 20th Century). Amazingly, the tighter money became, the more people came to the resort.

Below are a sample of contemporary newspaper reports from various quarters, which serve to show just how highly esteemed Blackpool and its Lights were at the period, the autumn event being all the more important now due to the fact that this was the first official evening switch-on by a personality. As the Hampstead Express reported, the personality in question was the very popular Lord Derby:

Young lads look on as the lamps are fitted to the 'Mary Mary' tableau of 1934.

"The most wonderful display of its kind in the country, the marvellous Blackpool Illuminations, now claim the attention of all who desire to combine a short visit to a bracing resort with the exhilaration of witnessing an electric display which is unrivalled for brilliance".

Other newspapers heaped equal praise on the event:

"The 1934 Blackpool Illuminations have begun. Before it ends, four weeks hence, probably two million autumn visitors will have seen the finest sea-front electrical display in the world". (Preston Guardian)

"The Blackpool Illuminations is a glowing and wonderfully planned harmony of colour – a town of changing stars, fireflies, and pillars of light". (Sunday Chronicle)

"No Lancashire cyclist should miss the Blackpool Illuminations, there is nothing to compare with it in Europe and, perhaps, in the world. It is not merely an illuminated town (such are common) it is the vastness and the scale of the thing". (Cycling)

"Lord Derby was obviously as thrilled by the beauty of the scene as any of the crowd when he switched on the 300,000 electric lamps. It is the biggest display Blackpool has had – and Blackpool had illuminations 50 years ago". (Sunday Graphic)

And here are Lord Derby's words on the subject:

> "The Illuminations at Blackpool have passed beyond the realm of local interest, they are known in all parts of the world. Let me express my admiration for the courage of those who have from year to year improved and increased this great spectacle".

Millions of people would echo his Lordship's very words. Blackpool had without doubt become a national institution and the resort was fulfilling its manifest destiny, which appeared to be that of bringing simple pleasures to many. The popularity of the lights was reflected in the staggering number of tram and bus passengers carried that year from April to October. The trams carried more than 34.5 million passengers, whilst the buses carried just over nine million; another amazing new record.

Joy and tragedy

For several reasons 1935 was a very busy year in the life of the town, despite the ever increasingly troubled world situation and perhaps even because of it. Whatever the reason, Blackpool's economy – though shaky – hadn't suffered to the same extent as many industrial towns and cities. Capital schemes undertaken by the council were keeping a proportion of the townsfolk occupied during the off-season months, whilst the showbiz people were valiantly doing their bit during the summer.

Much new roadwork and maintenance was being implemented, with a massive drainage scheme at the northern end of the borough; a new clubhouse was constructed at the ever improving Stanley Park.

Other council business centred on the Stanley Park airport. The latest Improvement Act contained a clause intended to curtail the obnoxious goings on along the Golden Mile which had led to numerous complaints over the years about the freak shows taking place there. The things that some people had found distasteful included the exhibition of Harold Davidson, the Rector of Stiffkey, defrocked due to allegations of immoral behaviour. This man had appeared on the Promenade for several years courtesy of the showman Luke Gannon, a man who made a small fortune on the Golden Mile. Little was spared in the pursuit of money, although it has to be said that Gannon was far from being on his own. The clause in the Act seems, however, to have made little impact as such things went on until at least the 1950s, due to the fact that Gannon and his contemporaries were somehow able to twist the facts and had their shows classed as waxworks exhibitions, which oddly were not included in the Act. Even the police were thwarted by this move when called in to close such shows. Eventually Davidson was exhibited again, this time threatening suicide if taken to court. He was arrested and charged with attempted suicide, but acquitted, only to come to a sticky end in Skegness when he was killed by a lion.

Other dubious acts on the Golden Mile over the years have included the world's biggest rat, which as it turned out was really a Mongoose, and Moby Dick the Whale, whose

A popular character, Fylde Ferdie was featured on several tableaux, one of which is shown here in 1938.

mummified body was displayed, mouth open, complete with a light bulb inside enabling the morbid and the curious to look inside its body cavity. Then there was the girl with the longest neck in the world; the ugliest woman in the world; several bearded ladies; the bride encased in a block of ice; and the Wolf Boy from Mexico. There was a young girl from Accrington who, despite being born without arms, could knit using her feet. There was a man supposedly 'crucified' with silver nails; a Midget called Alf Pyott, who was less than two feet high, and a man who defied death by having thousands of volts of electricity pumped into his body. There were a whole host of other sideshows, including what was alleged to be the chair that Napoleon used whilst in exile at St Helena, plus of course the 'hoopla' stalls, and the like. The many 'spielers', including an Australian known as 'the Admiral', tempted the vast crowds into these weird and wonderful shows.

Of course there were hundreds of slot machines and fruit machines available; there were also the 'smudge' artists (photographers), fortune tellers, weight guessers, ice cream vendors, rock sellers, fish and chip stalls, pubs and cafes galore. And in later years the candy floss purveyors, and 'kiss me quick' hat sellers, and the odd pickpocket of course. The list of attractions that have graced the Golden Mile over the decades is exhaustive, the above representing merely a sample. Perhaps the most popular of all though were the song booths operated by Lawrence Wright. These places had no ulterior motive, and for a few pence one could indulge in recording ones own voice, or purchasing a song sheet containing the latest hits; innocent fun and all watched over by the 'sands bobby' on his beat.

At the Tower, there was the annual crowning of the Cotton Queen, this year's lucky recipient of the title being Edna Taylor of Oldham. At the ceremony it seemed as though the whole of Oldham was there to cheer her on; nothing unusual in that though, as it often seemed that all of Oldham was in Blackpool.

Not to be outdone, the railway companies followed suit and chose as their Queen, a young lady by the name of Audrey Mosson, who on this occasion actually switched on the lights. At one time the Corporation operated a specially converted open topped bus for such events!

Meanwhile disaster struck during an air circus run by the famous flyer Sir Alan Cobham; several stunts were being performed over the town including 'wing walking', when two of the aircraft collided. One of the planes was able to land safely, but the second fell onto the town, killing the two women passengers and pilot. The plane and passengers fell to earth in Swainson Street, where the undercarriage smashed into the roof of a small boarding house, with the remainder falling onto Cedar Square. Although this was a tragedy, it's a wonder that it hadn't happened before. There had been much flying at Blackpool since the earliest days, resulting in only a few fatal crashes, and in a way even this crash was a something of a miraculous escape, for had the plane landed a hundred yards westwards, then it might well have ploughed into the thousands of spectators, who were enjoying the show.

Summer gave way to autumn, and the Lights once more shone with their accustomed brilliance; several new features had been added including a much higher proportion of animated tableaux. At the Tower and the Pleasure Beach there was even more coloured lighting than usual, with neon – the latest craze – much in evidence. Strip lighting was particularly suitable to highlight the modernistic new features at the amusement park, designed by the notable architect Joseph Emberton. Perhaps the finest example of his work there was the Fun House, possibly the biggest in the world.

The Lights crowds were, as usual, vast. And although the spending power per capita was down as before, the sheer weight of numbers went some way towards balancing the redress. Once again the tramways broke all records for passengers, as did the taxi cabs and the buses. The huge number of fares collected helped stave off financial ruin for the town, and helped prepare the way for next season. Typical Blackpool that! Always next season to look forward to, and almost before anyone realised, lo and behold the next season had arrived.

The world situation was, by now, deteriorating fast, with many pundits forecasting another war. Blackpool not only attempted to turn its back on such things, it actually sent a high powered delegation to tour the continent in an aeroplane named 'The Spirit of Blackpool'. Apparently the object of the exercise was to advertise the joys of the resort, though just what business they hoped to generate in Nazi Germany and Austria provides food for thought; after all, the town's *raison d'etre* was not war, it was to bring a little magic and colour into the humdrum lives of working people.

With this in mind the 1936 season got under way with a swing; George Formby topped the bill at the Opera House, Harry Korris starred at the South Pier, in conjunction with the Arcadian Follies, and at the Central Pier there was, as usual, a big cast that included the Royal Follies (note, no mention of Pierrots now!). Completing the trio at the North Pier was the old standby of 'On with the Show'. The Tower had its circus and ballroom dancing, whilst the

The 'Hickory Dickory Dock' tableau of 1932 was one of the first to include animation. A sequential controller was used to make the mouse and pendulum move.

An amusing tableau in which a gentleman foolishly stands in front of a dart board and gets his comeuppance in the company of 'Fylde Ferdie', the star of several comical scenes. This 1938 view of the Depot also includes a few electric fountains stacked up against the wall.

Winter Gardens carried on as before, dancing in the Empress Ballroom being as popular as ever.

As the season progressed in this, the 60th year of Blackpool's incorporation as a borough, the Illuminations were being erected as was the norm, but there was a big difference this year. In January, the Tramways Department had split from the Illuminations, having of course been under the same umbrella for years.

Charles Furness, the Manager for both departments, had retired in January and his assistant, Freddie Field, now elevated to Manager of the Illuminations Department, had suggested that the joint operations should be split in two. Accordingly, the Council agreed that they would give it a try and after a successful season it was decided to make the move permanent, and Field remained in sole charge of the operation for several years. The immediate problem faced by the new Department, now housed at Rigby Road, was one of severe financial cutbacks. A permanent staff of only around a dozen, including Field (but which it was agreed might rise to as many as 100 at the peak period, the men being temporarily on hire from other Council departments), now had to produce an annual show on a small budget. And, despite previous claims that the tramways were subsidising the lights, Field had now to show that the displays were not only self supporting, but were a feature that generated an enormous amount of money for the town as a whole.

As stated, the Department faced severe cutbacks because of the general financial situation, so they had to come up with new ideas at little cost. One of the ideas that was eventually used entailed the use of an old fire engine situated at the end of Central Pier. The object of the exercise was to pump jets of water high into the air, whilst at the same time playing huge coloured searchlights onto the streams of water, each powered by its own generator, and, according to newspaper reports of the day, this simple, cheap and effective feature was well received by the public. The actual switch-on of the Lights was performed by Sir Josiah Stamp who, acting in his capacity of Chairman of the LMS Railway Company, sent a radio signal from onboard a moving train, which tripped the switch and turned on the Lights. It was fitting that Josiah Stamp had switched on the 1936 Lights, because in that year the railways had brought a total of 900,000 passengers to the town during the six weeks of the Illuminations. Railways were now critical to the success of Blackpool Illuminations.

New for 1936 on the Bispham Cliffs was 'Fylde Ferdie', a comic character who was seen in a variety of situations with his trust dog, Fido.

Summer shows and Illuminations apart, the most spectacular event of the year was the burning down of the Boots store on Corporation Street, just behind the Town Hall, on 7th October. Many tens of thousands of pounds worth of damage occurred and a generation of council records went up in smoke. But the biggest price paid by far was the tragic death of one of the firemen. The unfortunate young man, Raymond Laycock, who, having only just returned to work after his honeymoon, was killed when working inside the building at the height of the blaze. This sad incident is commemorated at Laycock Gate, Layton, where a little street in the locality was renamed specifically in his honour. All in all a bad end to a year that had started with high optimism all round. But perhaps next season might be better!

High Hopes!

1937 blew in with the usual January gale, followed by rain, ice and snow. Eventually the winter petered out and soon spring was in the air and by the time the May blossom was out, Sir Josiah Stamp had been made the latest recipient of the freedom of the Borough. He was now actually to be known as Baron Stamp. And if that auspicious occasion wasn't enough, though, on 6th May that year, the town and the country celebrated the Coronation of King George VI and Queen Elizabeth. At the Town Hall there were celebrations attended by the good and the great. It was a joyous and moving occasion, especially given the abdication of Prince Edward, but it was played out against the ever deteriorating world situation.

Features being prepared for the Coronation of King George VI in 1937.

The summer shows were soon under way, more or less offering the mixture as before. Many of the old standbys were being trotted out yet again, with little new on offer. George Formby topped the bill again at the Opera House, whilst at the Grand Theatre, Gracie Fields starred once more.

Perhaps some of the most interesting events of the season were the several visits made by the media organisation known as 'Mass Observation' who, under their 'Worktown Project',

followed the daily lives of Bolton people. The results of these filmed visits were extremely interesting, showing the people of Bolton at work, rest and play, and showing life in Blackpool at the height of the season. Filming continued for several years, only being curtailed by the War.

Another major fire affected the resort on 27th August, when the Luna Park arcade on the Golden Mile was totally destroyed; only quick work by the fire brigade rescuing people from adjoining properties averted a dreadful disaster. This was actually the second such fire within a three week period at the establishment, the first having been caused by electrical failure. In fact the site was blighted by fire. Reads Market, occupying the site a generation earlier, was also similarly burned down.

By autumn, the lights were in place and were just waiting for the big switch-on, the event by now having become a major attraction in its own right, with thousands gathered at Talbot Square in joyful anticipation. The event this year was a rather strange affair, as the Lights were first switched on by Alderman Ashton, only to be switched on again on 21st October by the Duke Of Kent, who was in town to officially open the latest section of promenade at Bispham. Having done his duty as switch operator, the Duke boarded a tram that was disguised as an illuminated lifeboat and was whisked away on a grand tour.

In 1937, the Department had decided to start to phase out the monotonous festoon lighting along the Promenade. This lighting dated from 1925 and, whilst it still made a good impression when the Promenade was viewed from the piers, more variety was needed for the increasing number of people who viewed the Illuminations from motor cars. Frederick Field's solution was to create an avenue of plywood laburnum trees, which would eventually stretch from Pleasure Beach to Central Station. These trees would become synonymous with the Illuminations for many years.

Due to the financial situation, the Lights were not quite as spectacular as usual; nevertheless huge crowds appeared to see them.

Achievements and calamity

War was most definitely in the air by the time 1938 dawned; in Spain the civil war continued apace, and now both the Germans and the Italians had become involved. Prime Minister Stanley Baldwin retired, only to be succeeded by Neville Chamberlain, who visited Germany in a vain attempt to appease Hitler.

Only fools or supreme optimists could choose to ignore the warning signals, but as neither the members of the council in Blackpool, nor those who ran the tourist industry in the resort were considered fools, then it has to be said that as usual Blackpool was running on high optimism. For not only were there big plans for the coming summer season, but the Corporation had recently announced a set of massive, forward-looking plans for major redevelopment. Perhaps after all, no one in the resort believed that a war was inevitable; therefore, as with the North Pier, it was a case of "On with the show, this is it!"

The Council had pressed on with a major building project, which saw the multi-storied bus station on Talbot Road completed. The new Technical College was formally opened by the Earl of Crawford and a new St Johns public market was established on King Street, replacing the earlier one at Market Street. Much new housing was also being undertaken, both private and council inspired. New shops were appearing in the town centre, where the massive new Woolworth store was under construction, as was Britain's very first Littlewoods store, situated on Church

Street. But all of this paled into insignificance compared to the colossal redevelopment plans released by the Council later in the year. An enormous triangle of land had been purchased by the Corporation, with the object of moving the town centre southwards, as far as Chapel Street, where a new Central railway station was to be built. It was also proposed to remove the gasworks and electricity works, widen Central Drive, whilst at the same time wiping many streets from the map and blitzing the Golden Mile out of existence. Sadly the scheme was doomed before it started.

The King and Queen visited the town this year. As one would expect, they were given a rousing reception. Later, there was another Royal visit when the Duke Of

Trees on the Promenade are a rare sight. Even during the day the Illuminations dominate the scene, as can be seen here in 1938.

A similar view by night in the same year. The angle at which the photograph was taken has made the Tower appear to vanish, while the illuminated windmill and arch feature prominently.

From 1913 to 1937 the entrance to the Pleasure Beach was dominated by the Casino building. Decorated all over with white lamps, it was an impressive sight and one of the first buildings on the Promenade to be illuminated.

Kent paid a flying visit. These occasions were now coming thick and fast it seemed, as were the occasions when Freemen of the borough were installed. This year's recipient was a great local benefactor, Sir Cuthbert Grundy, of Grundy Art Gallery fame, a worthy choice if ever there was one!

As usual the summer season was under way; as before it was much of the same as the live theatres struggled to pay their way, and as cinema came more and more to the fore. The Golden Mile continued to offer its usual fare, and the Pleasure Beach went from strength to strength. However, although the amusement park was prospering and new attractions were constantly being added, there was a disastrous event there when the new Art Deco Casino building, now under construction, partially collapsed, killing and injuring several building workers. As if that wasn't bad

The illuminated gardens and cascades between Gynn Square and Uncle Tom's Cabin were one of the most attractive points on Blackpool's Promenade, as seen here in 1937.

The 'Prehistoric Blackpool' tableau of 1938 gives a humorous view of how the town would have looked with a wooden tower and hotels made from boulders.

enough there was another major fire, this time on the North Pier, where the Pavilion was totally destroyed.

Away from all of this, though, the Illuminations were in for a very big overhaul. In fact, the latest plans were easily the most ambitious ever and included so many new features that it would be impossible to relate them here due to lack of space. Some of the proposals were: a new 'Norway' theme at the Open Air Baths; coloured fountains at the paddling pools on the South Promenade; illuminated tram shelters; and St Chads Road was to have five searchlights in a fan design, in conjunction with a 'sky feature' and a double arch. The same was proposed for Manchester Square.

Also at Manchester Square would be a new tableau depicting Jack and Jill, whilst at Central Pier, there would be floodlit cascades of water. At the Central Railway Station and at the Town Hall there would be 'improved' features. Further north, there were several features in the pipeline, including the Two Cats Arch at the middle walk, more floodlighting and two new pylon features at the sunken gardens. On the cliffs there were to be several new tableaux, one of which was named 'Reflection', another called 'Pre-Historic' and yet another in the form of a ship and entitled 'Scream of the North'. Improvements to existing features were planned, including to a tableau named 'November the 5th'. Other proposed tableaux were entitled 'Stone Age', and finally there was to be a feature showing a magician, known as the 'Illusionist'. There were also many new futuristic looking illuminated pylons at various points along the Promenade, including a pair adjacent to Uncle Tom's Cabin, and at Cocker Square several illuminated fountains were due to glow.

Lytham Road, Central Drive, and Poulton Road were all designated to receive welcome arches, and to be more brightly lit than before, as was the case at Starr Gate. A new welcome arch was also planned for Queens Drive. The Town Hall was in line for lavish treatment, as was the shelter in the Square, this was to be highlighted

Below left: **Blackpool Tower has been subject to many illuminated designs. This 1938 view shows a zigzag and spiral effect.**

Below right: **Repairing features on the Promenade in 1938.**

Above: **Not all the tableaux were sited on the cliffs. This tulip field scene was appropriately sited beneath the windmill on Central Promenade in 1938.**

Left: **"Excuse me officer, what time do the Lights switch on?" The larger-than-life appeal of the Illuminations has had many children in awe over the years. This picture was taken in 1938.**

with the latest in neon strip lighting. Along the Promenade the majority of existing features would be upgraded and an avenue of cone pylons erected all the way from the North Pier as far south as the Palatine Hotel. There were also to be several imitation illuminated trees forming an avenue on one section of the Promenade.

These were the main features of the 1938 Illuminations. One thing that should be noted was that the director, Mr Freddie Field, and his team had planned even more new and bigger features but, working within constraints, they had actually held some back, hoping to introduce them all eventually.

Most of the proposals were, in fact, carried out and as Mrs Quayle, the wife of a Blackpool councillor pulled the switch, the lights burst into life. Accordingly the display was judged to be a fantastic achievement by all, especially considering the very tight budget. The public again flocked to the resort by rail; during the four week period more than 476,000 came by train, with many more arriving by car and coach than ever before. Once more the lights had saved the day, as the main season had turned out to be a rather dismal affair. Still, there was always next season to look forward to!

8 The lights go out over Europe!

The 'stick men', seen here in 1939, were responsible for making sure that wiring and lamps were fitted on the Tower. Working without the aid of a harness, a head for heights was essential.

The people of Blackpool were looking forward to a season that would make up for some of the disappointments of the previous year. However, several bad omens had been pointing to a less than rosy future and, as if that wasn't bad enough, yet another fire blighted the town. This fire was at, of all places, the Electricity Works on West Caroline Street, which had served the town since the era when the very first arc lamps were lit. Now merely a distribution centre within the National Grid, the works relayed electricity generated at Preston. As a consequence of the fire, the main switch room was completely burnt out, causing some disruption to service during a cold and very bleak week. This was to be a year of fires and mishaps!

Fires and mishaps apart, the season soon got underway. All the main venues such as the theatres and the cinemas were raring to go, as were majority of hotels and boarding houses in the town; cafes, restaurants, shops, pubs and clubs were fully stocked in anticipation of the annual Wakes Week crowds.

Buses, taxis, landaus and trams were all in pristine condition, as were the sailing vessels belonging to the local boatmen. Donkeys on the beach were in good form after their winter out to grass and their annual RSPCA inspection, and the Punch and Judy men were banging their drums in expectation of huge crowds who, with a bit of luck, would put money into their hats.

The Golden Mile was ready and waiting, freak shows, 'smudge' artists, cockles and mussels and all; each business hoping to become just a little more golden thanks to the holidaymaker. At the Pleasure Beach, and on the piers, it was the same story, as it was with those who manufactured and sold ice cream and of course the famous Blackpool rock! 'Fly pitchers' were everywhere, selling sun glasses, dodging the beady eye of the 'sands bobby'. Postcard sellers were well stocked; even the Post Office stocked up with extra stamps due to the expected posting of several million postcards. Along the prom, the massed ranks of newly refurbished deckchairs were lined up, ready and waiting for the thousands who would want to hire a seat for the day.

The young lads who, for a small fee, carried the bags from the railway and coach stations on behalf of the staying visitor, had repaired their home made trolleys, pram wheels being in desperately short supply. An army of local seasonal workers were now bolstered by an equally large army of seasonal workers from out of town, who came in anticipation of earning a small fortune in tips. Almost the whole town was geared up to cater to the mass of tourists, who between them might well total over ten million. As usual the Illuminations Department staff were working hard in order to get the lights ready for the autumn season, with plans being well in hand to introduce yet more of the proposed lighting features.

The Joseph Emberton designed Casino building was opened on 26th May 1939, and has become one of the symbols of the Pleasure Beach. It included new luxuries including full air conditioning. It was significantly modernised in 1977 and renamed the 'Wonderful World Building'.

All in all then, fires and mishaps apart, it appeared that Blackpool's future was looking better, especially so when one considers the huge capital spending rolling programmes implemented by the Council. New and wider roads were being created within the extended Borough and miles of new and improved sewers were under construction. Slum dwellings were being demolished, in tandem with the rapid expansion of social housing schemes. A new larger Victoria Hospital was under construction at Whinney Heys Farm, and the new Stanley Junior School had just been completed at Marton. On the North Promenade the Council had completed the magnificent Derby Baths, possibly the biggest indoor pool in the world, and on the South Promenade they had almost completed the Solarium building.

At the Pleasure Beach the magnificent Casino Building, which had so recently collapsed with a resulting sad loss of life, was at last completed, a credit to its builders. Stanley Park and its lovely golf course were looking as pretty as a picture, many of its trees and bushes now firmly established. Many bowling greens had been made ready for the season and the dog-racing track was also in tip-top condition (as, of course, were the competitors).

At Bloomfield Road the football ground was being readied for the coming season, the turf being in good shape despite the early season Football League Jubilee Charity Match between the Pool and Preston North End. Whilst at Stanley Park, the cricket team were going great guns challenging for honours in the Ribblesdale League.

On Dickson Road the town saw the construction of the largest Odeon Cinema ever, with a seating capacity in excess of 3,000. One of the first films shown there being the western classic 'Stagecoach', starring John Wayne.

There was also a new Opera House built to replace the former theatre at the Winter Gardens complex, its auditorium seating over 3,000 patrons in complete luxury, the feature being 'Turned out Nice Again' starring George Formby. Cinemas were showing the latest features, including 'Gunga Din' at the Palace and 'The Gang's All Here' with Jack Buchanan at the Hippodrome. There was a new pavilion on the North Pier, a replacement for the one previously destroyed by fire. Here audiences were treated to 'On with the Show', while at the Central Pier there was roller skating and the 'Royal Follies'.

Yet more new features for the Illuminations were under construction by the staff at the Rigby Road depot, led by Freddie Field. These included the giant Canadian scenery at the Open Air Baths. This feature was in commemoration of the Royal visit by King George VI and Queen Elizabeth the previous year (1938). Miles of wiring had been installed by the small army of technicians employed by the Lights department and who, due to the exceptionally large crowds and the dense motor traffic, had been forced to work throughout the night on several occasions in order to complete their task. Their task included the placing of several hundred thousand bulbs, each tested, polished, and then screwed home. The installation of more than fifteen miles of strip lighting had also been undertaken in readiness for the upcoming switch-on.

Even before the switch-on it was reported that Blackpool had recently consumed more electricity than at any previous time in its history. The increase over the same period the previous year being at least 15 per cent, possibly due to the fact that more and more people were buying household appliances, plus of course there were many new buildings in the town, the majority of which were now fitted with electric lighting.

Not all was well with the world, however, for as the drumbeat of war grew ever nearer and ever louder, a series of mishaps hit the town.

On 26th April, there was yet another fire at the Pleasure Beach, and on 30th May, the popular Imperial Cinema on Dickson Road was engulfed in flames; the building's interior was utterly devastated, the probable cause being electrical failure. At the Pleasure Beach, the Indian Theatre was totally gutted and the Ice Drome was severely damaged; but one of the biggest shocks of all was yet to come.

At approximately 2.45am, on 26th August, there was a shattering explosion that was heard up to five miles away. A bomb, believed to have been placed by the IRA, had exploded outside the Town Hall. Having been placed at the north east corner of

Above: **The Opera House in 1939.**

Right: **The new Pavilion on Blackpool's North Pier.**

the building, the bomb exploded with such a force that it smashed the thick iron railings. Although the brickwork and stonework suffered only a limited amount of damage, several beautiful stained glass windows were wrecked, as were many others in Talbot Square. Illumination features, which were in the process of being installed there, were also badly damaged. A search of the town centre revealed several more unexploded bombs; two were in a dustbin at the rear of the Woolworth store and the Tower, whilst another was found in the grounds of the Police Station at Albert Road. This bomb was made up of several sticks of gelignite, which if detonated would have caused enormous damage to the building, and quite possibly resulting in serious loss of life.

The Grand Pavilion, South Pier, in 1949.

All of this happened at the busiest part of Blackpool's season where, even in these abnormal times, all the planning had come together and the expected huge crowds had materialised. In fact, they were even bigger than anticipated and the season was going extremely well, despite the apparent forebodings. However, it was doomed to quickly fizzle out due to the rapidly worsening state of events on the Continent, which was already in the throes of war, the Germans now having invaded Poland.

War was announced in Blackpool on 3rd September, just a few days before the Illuminations were due to be switched on for the autumn. In fact the Lights were actually fully lit as a dress rehearsal, but for one night only, then immediately switched off again, not to be seen again for another ten long years.

The staff from the Illuminations Department were ordered to dismantle the whole system, even removing the lamps from the public lights in the streets. Their next task was to assist in the digging of air raid shelters along the cliff tops, where so recently they were engaged in erecting the lights tableaux, the materials of which went piece by piece to the war effort. The ex-naval search lights that had been a feature of the Illuminations were now commandeered for service by the War Office, being sent to various ports in the south of England, and some even being sent to the small resort town of Barry Island, South Wales.

Although there is no record of just how many of these lights found their way to Barry Island, it is reasonably safe to state that at least some of Blackpool's lights shone there during the hostilities, even though those who bravely operated them probably hadn't a clue!

At war again

A season that had promised so much now fizzled out completely, the rest of the year being a complete waste of time as far as the tourist trade was concerned. The Tower Company glumly announced a 90% drop in takings compared with the previous year when the Lights were in action. By the time January 1940 came around the weather took a hand and massive snowdrifts blocked the roads for weeks on end as the temperature plummeted to an all time low. And things were looking even gloomier as the Government announced that butter and bacon were to be rationed, although

With the country facing the prospect of war, Illuminations staff were transferred to building air-raid shelters all over town. This view shows members of the Illuminations team digging shelters on the cliffs in 1939.

initially many of the larger local grocers and butchers, such as Booths, Redmans, Melias and the Co-op, advertised that they held big stocks and saw no immediate problems, so there was no need to panic, which of course people did.

The problems multiplied quickly as thousands of troops were billeted in the town and once again most of larger hotels were requisitioned for the purpose. These men and women came from every corner of the British Isles, as well as from Australia, New Zealand and Canada, and eventually from Poland, France and America too. The town was turned into a giant garrison, training troops of every branch of the armed forces, but particularly so for the RAF, which established its training headquarters in the town. Perhaps as many as 150,000 such troops were trained in and around Blackpool, the town being ringed with airfields such as those at Kirkham, Weeton and Stanley Park, where the airport was commandeered and used for the RAF's parachute training exercises. Squires Gate airport was also commandeered and here giant new runways were installed and a huge aircraft manufacturing facility built. This factory reportedly had the largest single span roof in the world. It was to collapse under construction, killing many construction workers and delaying the project. Eventually it was finished, and by the end of the War the factory had turned out more than 4,000 Wellington bombers.

Squires Gate remained fully operational throughout the War. There were several squadrons of Spitfires and Hurricanes based there, not primarily for the defence of Blackpool; on the contrary, they were there to help protect Liverpool and Manchester. The Airport was attacked on several occasions, but mainly with incendiaries, which is rather surprising due to the fact that after the War, the Allies discovered high level German reconnaissance photographs that clearly showed that the enemy knew exactly what activity was taking place there. The question is, therefore, why did they not bombard the factory?

The town also became the training centre for the RAF's School of Wireless Telegraphy and several other branches concerning flying operations. Amongst the trainees drafted into the resort were entertainers such as Max Bygraves who, as a professional after the War, came back time and time again to star in the resort's theatres, as did several of his comrades, including Cyril Fletcher, Max Wall and Eric Barker. Notable musicians in the RAF at Blackpool included Norrie Paramour, and Sydney Torch.

Quite apart from the thousands of servicemen billeted in the town there were tens of thousands of evacuees; mainly, but not exclusively, young children. All of these people, along with several thousand others who were sent to Blackpool to work, were housed in hotels, boarding houses, private homes and anywhere else that could accommodate them. This situation caused quite a lot of friction, especially when the Government decreed that evacuees must be housed.

Digging in for victory

As the town settled down for a long war it became obvious that the Illuminations would not be seen again for a considerable period; in addition to this, due to the total blackout imposed, the resort was having more than a little difficulty operating at anything like normal.

The sudden increase in the town's population obviously put the services in the town under immense strain, especially so later in the War, when food, petrol and power rationing really kicked in. Although it is true to say that no one in the town starved, there were many who struggled to get by on a meagre diet and, had it not been for the various social programmes and local charities, the situation could have been much worse. A thriving black market may have made money for the few unscrupulous 'spivs', but it certainly didn't help the poor families who sometimes suffered badly.

Within a short space of time, though, the Government introduced a policy of 'Dig for Victory'; every available plot of land that could be utilised for growing crops was brought into action. The local Council made available many plots of land for allotments; these were available to all at a modest rent of ten shillings a year and went a long way towards alleviating the situation. Similarly, people were encouraged to keep chickens in their back gardens, although cockerels were frowned upon for obvious reasons. In order to promote such schemes, Freddie Field, boss of the Illuminations Department, was asked to design unlit tableau-style backdrops demonstrating the benefits of growing one's own food. As a result of his team's efforts, the Town Hall and other prominent buildings were surrounded by these tableaux, some of which asked people to support the war effort by saving scrap metal and the like, whilst others asked people to dig deeply into their pockets and give money for arms. Obviously this form of activity was a necessary kind of propaganda, but who could have ever foreseen the day when the Illuminations Department would be so involved?

Below left: **Here is an example of an unilluminated tableau from the war years. 'Wings for Victory' was displayed at the Town Hall between 1939 and 1945.**

Below right: **Soldiers stand in front of 'Junk Week', another unilluminated tableau. The public were asked to help with all the scrap they could spare. This picture dates from 1941.**

Big band bonanza!

Dances were especially popular in wartime and many top bands, especially military ones such as the Squadronairres, played at the Tower, the Palace and the Winter Gardens, where the ever popular Charlie Barlow and Charles Farrell also appeared on many occasions. Other big names to appear were Geraldo, Vera Lynn, Jack Hylton and, of course, the inimitable Joe Loss.

The theatres played their part admirably, featuring top shows starring well known artistes whenever available. The Palace featured names such as Norman Evans, Billy Nelson and Duggie Wakefield. North Pier featured the old favourite 'On with the Show', and Feldman's produced a show entitled 'It'll Be Reight', starring Roy Barbour. But the cinemas possibly played the biggest role of all, opening their doors as early as possible during the day, whilst showing films on a more or less continual basis (although, due to the blackout, everywhere had to close by 10pm). One popular film showing at the Princess was the great Edward G Robinson's, 'Confessions Of A Nazi Spy'. Blackpool Football Club played their part too; in fact they won major honours in the necessarily modified league, with many top class professionals from the ranks of the RAF featuring as guest players. All along the Promenade, except perhaps during air raids, the entertainments and stalls were open. Even though many everyday items were not available people were determined to enjoy themselves wherever possible. On a sunny day the crowds along the Promenade and the beach could easily have been mistaken for peacetime crowds, were it not for the many uniforms on display. So busy were the beach donkeys that the Council issued a charter designed for their health and welfare. It seems that overweight and overzealous individuals were making life hard for the poor little animals.

Light at the end of the tunnel

Eventually the war was won and Attlee's Labour Government ousted Winston Churchill, who soon became Blackpool's latest Freeman. With the peace being won, the citizens of Great Britain, along with the returning troops, were hoping that life could get back to normal as quickly as possible. These were forlorn hopes, however, as food rationing became even more stringent. There were massive housing shortages and all manner of things were in short supply. Things like household goods, cars, motorbikes and cycles were almost impossible to obtain, even if one could afford to buy them.

All of this affected Blackpool greatly. Boarding houses, cafes and hotels struggled to put on a menu, utilising whatever everyday vegetables could be procured, along with powdered eggs, Spam fritters and a horrible fish called Snook. This wasn't helped when a big fire at North Station destroyed thousands of tea rations. But, of course, the black market throve and the term 'under the counter' became a byword and, providing that one had the ready money, many exotic products became available. Blackpool was a hotbed of such activity, with many well-known and highly respected people becoming involved. Without getting into the politics of this, sadly this is what war and its aftermath does to a country.

At this time Blackpool was once again stuck in deep snowdrifts and in the grip of icy temperatures, which saw it struggling to get back on its feet. The Government brought in measures that would create the National Health Service, nationalise the railways, and nationalise the electricity industry, amongst many others. These swingeing measures were vital if the country was ever to get back on an even keel.

But from the point of view of resorts such as Blackpool, they were hardly designed to get things moving once more as primarily they were designed for industry getting the first call on raw materials and fuel. Coal was in extremely short supply and, of course, still rationed, as was electrical power. The result of this was there were frequent power cuts, some of which occurred without warning. Many factories were struggling to cope with these conditions, and of course these things were reflected in every day life.

Despite the shortages and the uncertainty of everything, the crowds rolled back into Blackpool, as large as, if not larger than, before. The theatres were much in demand, and all the usual

Blackpool Tower and Golden Mile in 1949.

stars were there including Josef Locke, Dave Morris and Cheerful Charlie Chester, amongst a host of others. Cinemas did their bit by showing many top line Hollywood features, including 'Gaslight', starring Ingrid Bergman, 'National Velvet', starring Elizabeth Taylor; and 'Till The Clouds Roll By', with Frank Sinatra and Judy Garland. Meanwhile, out at Stanley Park, the town was featuring the Royal Agricultural Show amongst its many attractions.

Somehow or another the enormous crowds of this rather austere era were catered for by the ingenuity of the Blackpool traders. Oranges and apples were sold for up to a half a crown each; where they came from no one seems to know! Meanwhile, down on the Golden Mile, traders were selling such items as 'kiss me quick' hats, fabricated from pre-war wallpaper fents. The Government pulled out all the stops to ensure that beer was available, although more exotic drinks were not so easily obtained and were very heavily taxed. Nevertheless, the day-tripper generally had a good time in Blackpool due, in many ways, to its marvellous beaches, promenade and piers, where even if one didn't have much to spend, a good time was almost freely available. Many thousands turned out to watch the Freedom of the Borough being conferred on the great Field Marshall Viscount Montgomery of Alamein, this affair just the latest of many such spectacles featuring military bands marching up and down the Promenade. Other free shows that excited the crowds were the frequent fires which occurred with amazing regularity during the decade, which included yet another blaze on the Tower structure and an even bigger fire at the Pleasure Beach that saw the Ice Drome severely damaged once again. Another free show was the crowds themselves, who attracted quite a lot of media attention. Indeed, crowd-watching was a worthwhile occupation, for all life passed by on Blackpool's famed Promenade and Golden Mile. One way or another, Blackpool was fulfilling its role as a 'lung' for the war weary nation.

The town was overjoyed when its football team reached the FA Cup Final for the first time ever, and even though they were beaten, things were definitely looking up in the resort. The one thing missing from the equation was the yearned for reintroduction of the Illuminations but, despite fervent pleas to the Government, the Council was informed that there was no spare electrical capacity with which to stage the show. In any case, Freddie Field, the lights chief, had retired and the Council had disbanded the Illuminations team and got rid of the majority of lighting equipment. It appeared that there was little hope for the lights after all.

All was not lost, however, as during 1949, following a fairly dramatic upsurge in the production of coal, and hence electricity, the Government relented, telling Blackpool Council that it might consider allowing them to stage the lights after all. Before such a decision could be made, and there were moments when it looked like the ministry might renege, many messages and telephone calls went to and fro between Blackpool and London. But at the final hour the go ahead was given, much to the joy and the relief of the town.

This was just the beginning, though, and there was a lot of hasty planning required before the town could even think of staging its autumn Illuminations once again. There were many hurdles to overcome but, as usual, Blackpool rose to the task!

Freddie Field was hurriedly brought out of retirement, given a small budget of around £1,000 and told to use as much of the remaining pre-war lights stock as humanly possible. There was one snag however; the Illuminations staff had been dispersed and, as a result, there were few technicians available with the required skills with which to affect the lights display. This resulted in Field making hurried calls to several previous staff members who formed the basis of a new work team augmented by about one hundred skilled and semi-skilled workers. Now they were in business!

By the time Anna Neagle – the celebrity invited for the switch-on at the Town Hall – arrived, the team had worked wonders in producing a massive spectacle that, although not quite up to scratch in some departments, was nevertheless a triumph.

Hundreds of special trains, buses, and coaches were laid on for the event. Private motorists miraculously appeared in bigger numbers than ever, possibly bringing in total well over 400,000 passengers to see the switch-on. Indeed, the crowds who packed into Talbot Square and lined the Promenade on that cool early autumn evening, were amongst the biggest the town had ever seen. Several million people came to Blackpool during the Lights, and when Anna Neagle threw the switch, causing the various sections of lights to come on, one by one, there was a deafening roar. This roar was a nation's way of showing its relief and emotion after enduring a decade of war and deprivation. Blackpool was serving its purpose in style!

The pre-war Cinderella tableau made a welcome return to the cliffs in 1949.

Back at last, this time for good

The 1949 display, although modest by modern standards, was large by pre-war standards and had been a huge success; the crowds that came to see the lights were amongst the largest ever to hit the resort, with over 800 weekend special trains bringing hundreds of thousands of trippers into town. Small wonder then that Mr W E Lister (Chairman, Hotels and Restaurants Association) commented:

"There has been nothing like it in Blackpool's Illuminations history. It has not been possible to meet all requests for accommodation."

Everywhere was fully booked and the Director of Publicity reported that as many as 1,680 postal enquiries for accommodation were received in one day, whilst tired visitors who had not been able to acquire accommodation walked several miles inland, knocking on doors of terraced homes where they pleaded for a bed for the night, even if that meant sleeping in the bath or the garden shed. Many of these requests were granted, putting a few extra shillings into the household kitty.

Pathe News screened a bulletin titled 'It's Blackpool no longer!', referring to the reintroduction of the Lights on the previously darkened Promenade. Surviving the War, favourite tableaux were seen once more, including the 'Golfers', 'Windmill', 'Babes in the Wood' and 'Rejuvenator'. The infamous 'Juggling Clowns' had also survived, their presence still bringing more than a flicker of a smile as people remembered the Clowns' moment of fame in 1932.

Below left: **Rejuvenator tableau, 1949.**

Below right: **The windmill on Central Promenade in 1949, complete with summer scene. The windmill remains in the display to this day.**

Since the introduction of tableaux in 1928, it had become customary to have an illuminated scene on the Town Hall. Originally the scene was of two golfers but then in 1932 it was decided to replace them with something different, namely two 'Juggling Clowns', which were displayed prominently on the Town Hall buildings. As a result the place was soon dubbed the 'Clown Hall', and members of the 52-strong Council were frequently asked, "Where are the other 50?" The answer soon became "they have gone to Bispham", as within a couple of weeks a Council meeting demanded their removal to the cliff tops. Soon after midnight, the clowns were secretly removed, or so the Council thought, for everyone in the town knew what had happened, making the Council the butt of even more jokes. The 'Golfers', whose presence was seen as more respectable, were re-installed at the Town Hall, from where an official statement said: "There is so much light in Talbot Square that the clown figures were not shown off to advantage and they have been removed to a darker background at Bispham." This didn't fool anybody; now even the Golfers seemed amused.

The 'Juggling Clowns' under construction in the Depot. The clowns would soon be displayed on the front of the Town Hall buildings, resulting in the building being jokingly dubbed the 'Clown Hall'.

New lights for a new age

Shortly after the closure of the 1949 lights season, Freddie Field retired for good, this time handing over the reins to Mr Harry Carpenter, who was to oversee the modernising of the street lighting and the whole of the Illuminations Department. With this task he was ably assisted by AS Howell (design), GL Winckley (technical), E Rathmell (electrical) and general assistant R Wilson.

Carpenter and his team would make changes to the Illuminations which would lay the foundations for the lights for the remainder of the century. By the time 1950 came around, Blackpool had 9,799 lamps of which 3,421 were electric (35%) and 6,378 were gas. From these figures it's easy to see that the early fears that gas would soon be a thing of the past were not yet realised, but Carpenter knew that the system needed to modernise, and modernise quickly.

The electric lights were mostly 100-500 watt tungsten filament lamps and 278-400 watt mercury vapour lamps. In re-planning the lighting, consideration had to be made for roadways totalling 275 miles in length, this mileage showing just how the town – the population of which was now well over 140,000 – had grown over the past 100 years. The choice of light source was mercury vapour. Tungsten had been eliminated due to its low luminous efficiency, and the colour given off by sodium was thought too garish in a seaside resort. Fluorescent lighting was also desirable as its light was softer and gave a more even spread, but due to cost it was reserved for special use.

Renewing the lighting on the Promenade was a feat in itself. The existing carriageway lighting consisted of canopies fixed on tramway standards along the footpath between the road and tramway and there was still an occasional gas lamp on the east side of the carriageway, including the Golden Mile. As the lights had grown in size and complexity, it had become

An early picture of Bispham Sub Station.

apparent that this system was inadequate; there were many occasions where the electrical system was unable to carry the load, resulting in blackouts. The new lighting had to be adaptable during the Illuminations, and several designs were considered before a scheme which incorporated tubular fluorescent lamps was chosen. This scheme allowed conical coloured screens to be fitted during the Illuminations.

Eleven substations were built along the Promenade, two of which were located on the cliffs where the load was the greatest. The west side poles, which were sited at 120 ft intervals along the Promenade during 1953/4, were of spun-concrete, which minimised the need for maintenance. They were also fitted with eyehooks to allow for attachment of festoon cables. At salient positions on the Promenade, green fluorescent lamps were fitted instead of coloured screens, the idea here being that on extremely busy evenings they would help the hard pressed, white-coated police to stand out at traffic control points.

Costing £55,000, the 1950 lights comprised 300,000 lamps and features were built using 10 tons of paint and 20 tons of wood. Keen to present a significantly 'new' display, Carpenter's team of 130 men – joiners, electricians, scenic artists, plasterers and labourers – worked solidly, presenting a display where a third of the tableaux

Above Left: **An early picture of Gynn Square Sub Station.**

Above Right: **An early picture of the Mercury Arc Sub Station at Copse Road, Fleetwood.**

(Blackpool Transport)

An illuminated wonderland: Noah's Ark and Hiram Maxim's Captive Flying Machine at the Pleasure Beach in 1951.

The 'New York Skyline' tableau of 1950 suffered badly at the hands of the weather, despite being supported by a huge amount of scaffolding.

were new features, including one giant scene that represented the 'New York Skyline'. At 120ft long and a costly £1,500 (£100,000 today), the Queen Mary ocean liner was shown entering the harbour, being described in the press as a "gesture to our American friends". Leaving nothing to chance, the tableau was held up by a mass of scaffolding, an impressive sight in itself. Despite all precautions, the weather brought down the tableau, causing sufficient damage to warrant a complete rebuild. It returned in 1951, complete with redesigned skyscrapers and the addition of John Bull and Uncle Sam, and a more wind-proof scaffolding assembly!

A nice little earner (to use Golden Mile parlance) for the Corporation was the hiring out of floodlighting equipment to hotels and boarding houses; this not only raised money, but also meant that there were extra Illuminations on display, this time paid for by the hotelier!

Beauty and Bovril!

In 1949 the Lights attracted over four million late season visitors, but by 1950 the figure had dropped to just over two million. And despite the talents of Wilfred Pickles, there wasn't enough money on the table; as a result a council meeting in January 1951 looked for ways to attract more visitors and other forms of funding the Lights.

The first idea considered was a nationwide beauty contest to be called 'Queen of the Lights'. The plan was to split the country into seven regions, each region having its area finals and regional finals. A grand final would then be held in Blackpool, with the winner being the first to switch on the Illuminations, whilst the other six would afterwards perform a switch-on ceremony during weekends most appropriate to the holiday periods of their regions. The Open Air Baths was an ideal location for the final, though later contests were held in the Illuminations Depot, where the opportunity was taken for beautiful girls to pose with the new features wearing little more than swimming costumes, a smile and a wink!

To ease the Lights' burden on the ratepayers, the Electrical Services Committee proposed to include advertisements in the Illuminations. Firms and advertising agencies were approached and interest was shown from various parties. By March 1951, two sites had been recommended to the Council – the car parks at Derby Baths and Gynn Square, where it was estimated the income from advertising at these two locations might be £1,000.

The scheme at Gynn Square was the more controversial of the two. Based on a view of London's Piccadilly Circus, the tableau included several adverts for large companies, and although impressive from the front, it was the view from the rear (or lack of it!) that led to a 100-strong petition being sent to the Town Clerk. Following on from experiments in 1950, masses of tubular scaffolding had been used to support the massive structure. Residents and landladies objected to losing their sea view, the latter also concerned that visitors were unable to see their establishments and so were losing trade as a result.

Above left: **Piccadilly advertisement, Gynn Square 1951.**

Above right: **The South Shore Baths were an ideal setting for the 'Queen of the Lights' beauty contests, shown here in 1955. The Baths also hosted illuminated tableaux during the autumn.**

Left: **'Bird Cage Walk' at the Cabin in 1951. Attached only at the top, the cages had to be tied back to the poles when winds were fierce.**

Plastic fantastic

1950 had seen the introduction of plastic to the Illuminations, being shaped into tulips, daffodils and other blooms, forming the carriageway section 'Concours des Fleurs'. The introduction of this themed section broke up the monotonous strings of festoon, further themed sections being added in 1951. 'Fantasia Walk' comprised coloured pylons and Venetian lanterns, but the main highlight was a section called 'Birdcage Walk'. Three-dimensional 10ft illuminated budgerigars, parakeets and other caged birds were made from a plastic that was sprayed onto a metal frame. In following years, the cacti of 'Arizona Avenue' and sea creatures of 'Mermaids Retreat' were also made from the sprayed plastic, the introduction of which had caused a minor sensation amongst the lights crowds.

The updating of the Illuminations continued apace in 1951. On the cliffs, half the tableaux were new features, including a Halloween scene, a 150ft Italian Garden and an Artist tableau, whilst Egyptian sand-dancers appeared for the first time at South Shore.

Below left: **Taken c.1950 this is an impressive picture of the gardens and Promenade between Gynn Square and Cabin. Besides the town centre, the Promenade had a few key places where special effort was made, this being one of them.**

Below right: **Although the Lights have been switched on, it doesn't mean work on the Promenade is over. Strict targets are set for achieving high levels of reliability, so crews patrol the Promenade constantly in search of faulty or unlit features.**

Blackpool, Television star!

A breakthrough in northern television broadcasting came on 12th October 1951 with the opening of the Holme Moss television transmitter, which at the time was the most powerful transmission station in the world. The station, planned by BBC engineers, boasted a mast soaring 750ft above the moors, 230ft higher than Blackpool Tower. At 8pm, the first outside television broadcast in the North of England showed the ceremony to mark the opening of the transmitter at Manchester Town Hall. Chairman of the governors of the BBC, Lord Simon, officially opened the station. Invited guests included "probably the most widely representative meeting of northern mayors that has ever been." Although that statement might have been challenged by Blackpool, which years earlier had witnessed the disgusting scandal when "fifty mayors were drunk" on the Promenade.

To commemorate the opening, special transmissions were planned from Blackpool, including a live screening of the Illuminations. Months of planning between BBC engineers, Blackpool's Transport and Illuminations Departments, Tower Company officials and Post Office engineers resulted in the Illuminations being seen from a converted tramcar. Former circular tour favourite Toastrack 165

A Souvenir of the Lights

The Council and local newspapers have, over the years, produced official souvenir guides to the Illuminations. As well as containing photographs of new features for that year, the guides also contain details about the display, attractions and events during the autumn months and a host of miscellaneous advertising.

Over the years, the Illuminations have become the feature of souvenirs in countless gift shops. As well as postcards, there have been tea towels, plates, badges, pens and many other themed items. For some people however, a small souvenir is not sufficient. These people have their eyes set on bigger and better items, the Illuminations themselves!

Surplus illuminations were sold off from time to time as enquiries came in, but for the first time, in 1953, a full catalogue of sale items was prepared. Illuminations Director Harry Carpenter had inherited an ageing collection of features upon his appointment in 1950 and, from that point, he set out to add new features. Whilst a few tableaux were 'recycled' and displayed in a different manner, after the insurgence of new features many pre-war tableaux were simply surplus to requirements. Blackpool's reputation for outstanding features soon tempted many other resorts, towns and cities to buy the retired tableaux. Unfortunately, a few of these towns then started boasting about 'their' illuminations and asked the question: "Why go to Blackpool when you can see Blackpool's Illuminations here?" Obviously far from amused, this incident led to the Illuminations Department changing their policy on the sale of withdrawn features. Overseas bidders were then given preferential treatment. Over the years, features have been sold to the city of Jeddah in Saudi Arabia, Barcelona and illuminated windmills even went to Holland!

Fortunately, the bid by Libyan Colonel Gaddafi's emissary to buy up the complete Illuminations, down to the last light bulb, failed. Blackpool wasn't prepared to give up its goose that laid the golden eggs.

When this leaflet was published in 1939 nobody really expected the Illuminations to be cancelled because of war.

Left: **Blackpool was proud to re-launch the illuminations in 1949, as can be seen from this leaflet publicising the event.**

Below: **Blackpool Gazette and Herald Ltd were responsible for the publication of many Illuminations souvenir guides. The designs were always very elaborate.**

(Andrew Hazlehurst Collection)

had cameras and transmitting equipment fitted, with the pick-up point being at the top of the Tower. The signals were then radioed to an intermediate station, then on to Manchester and from there, by cable to the new transmitting station at Holme Moss.

On Sunday 14th October 1951 at 8pm, television came to Blackpool. Speaking from a room at the Miners' Convalescent Home, 'sandgrown' Mr H Douglas Bickerstaffe, the chairman of the Tower and Winter Gardens companies, addressed the nation with the line: "It is my pleasure to welcome television to Blackpool." Mr Bickerstaffe was the first Blackpool man to be televised from the town, which was fitting, as his father Alderman Tom Bickerstaffe had played a principal role in bringing about the Illuminations, and of course his uncle John had built the Tower! After a short interview with announcer Sylvia Peters, attention was then switched to the South Shore, where the television tram was waiting. (Not only was this the first live televised broadcast from an English seaside resort, but within a handful of years Blackpool FC and Bolton Wanderers took part in the first ever live broadcast of an English soccer match, and the Tower was the setting for what may well have been the first live screening of a boxing match in England). Television had taken Blackpool to its bosom, but eventually the town would pay a price for this!

As well as the crew and BBC technicians, on board was announcer David Southwood who made an excellent job of describing the splendour of the colourful Illuminations to the families watching at home in black and white (no such thing as televised snooker then!) Wilfred Pickles presented a half hour show from the Miners' Home and then attention went back to the Illuminations as the tram reached the tableaux.

On the last night of the Illuminations, a Ministry of Fuel and Power licence came into force, prohibiting the use of lighting for advertising purposes and shop window displays until after 7pm, almost a case of *déjà vu*. To quash ill feeling, the 5.31pm planned switch-on time was put back to 7pm.

In a progressive and daring move, Blackpool actually made tableaux to be displayed in other cities. In 1951, a Leeds railway station was home to a tableau advertising the Illuminations. During the day, promenade views painted in phosphorescent colours could be seen, whilst at night, ultra-violet ray lamps brought the scene to life, creating an attention-grabbing view.

Mickey's trip to the Moon scene, 1952.

Towards the end of 1951, big plans were drawn up for a 50ft long and 17ft high tableau promoting Blackpool, with three scenes depicting the Promenade, Stanley Park, and the Pleasure Beach with South Shore Baths. The slogan, 'Blackpool, World's Playground', adorned the central panel. It was planned to display the tableau in Euston Road, London, between Euston and St. Pancras railway stations. Whether the plans came to fruition is unclear.

Cartoon capers

In a surprise announcement on 11th December 1951, Harry Carpenter described how negotiations were in place with the Disney organisation for their involvement in the 1952 Illuminations. The design work would be undertaken by Disney, with the construction work completed, as ever, by the

Seven Dwarfs scene, 1952.

Illuminations Department. The agreement benefited both parties – Blackpool got to use Disney's characters and Disney got free publicity for their films. Many new features had a Disney theme, including the carriageway section 'Kartoon Kollonade', a 200ft long tableau called 'Mickey's Trip To The Moon' and another called 'Christmas Party'. Other older features were adapted, including the ever-popular 'Blackpool Rejuvenator', which now featured Disney characters. For twenty years, many of Disney's film releases became illuminated tableaux, both cartoon and live-action; one cannot help but wonder whether Walt Disney knew of all this free publicity (although pundits at the time called for the whole show to be put into the hands of the Walt Disney Corporation).

Luminous legalities

By 1952, the ever-increasing cost of the Illuminations was causing concern amongst some private residents who claimed they got no benefit from the Illuminations and were aggrieved that the Lights were being financed out of the rates. It was also suggested that subsidising the Lights from the rates could be illegal; although the Council already had powers to allocate money for the benefit and improvement of the town, they needed to obtain unquestionable powers to use ratepayers' money. To offset some of the costs, the Council wanted the right to close Stanley Park and Middle Walk on the Promenade, illuminate them with superior displays and then charge for admission. These rights were given in the 'Blackpool Corporation Act 1952', but in fact were never implemented.

In a retrospective move, Parliament also conferred on Blackpool the inalienable right to provide Illuminations, so that now after 40 years the funding and operations concerning the Illuminations were absolutely legal.

Queen Elizabeth's Coronation was celebrated in grand style in 1953. The Promenade was decorated from South Pier to Gynn Square with bunting, shields and

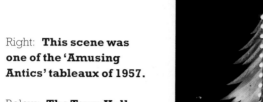

Right: **This scene was one of the 'Amusing Antics' tableaux of 1957.**

Below: **The Town Hall was illuminated extravagantly for the Coronation in 1952. Note the spire, which, sadly, is no longer a feature, having been damaged in a storm.**

600 Union Jacks and Dominion Flags. The Tower bore a crest on the seaward side consisting of a 15ft by 9ft crown and 'ER' in 12ft letters. On the Promenade opposite the Tower was a set of tableaux, including two representing each of the Elizabeths. These were joined by horse guards, heralds and Coronation figures. An 11ft by 8ft picture of the Queen graced the Town Hall and pylons bearing crowns were erected along Central Promenade. Tram shelters too were topped with 8ft by 5ft crowns and tram standards featured shields and coats of arms. The trams themselves were fitted with illuminated shields and crowns. The illuminated 'Progress' tram bore the message, "Health unto Her Majesty. Long May She Reign", written out in lamps covering one side of the car, together with flags, crowns and the letters 'ER'. The other side bore the message: "Welcome to our visitors by land, sea and air". Altogether 6,000 coloured lamps (many red white and blue!) were used on the tram. As usual Blackpool had gone over the top!

1953 was a memorable year for Blackpool in many ways. After watching Blackpool FC win the FA Cup by four goals to three against Bolton at Wembley in one of the most remarkable comebacks of all time, Harry Carpenter decided that a tableau would be built to commemorate the event. He even drew the rough design for it on his way home! The design

included a giant Tower and FA Cup with faces, as well as photographs of the winning team. This match incidentally saw Stan Mortensen of Blackpool score the first and only Wembley hat trick.

The efforts of Blackpool FC and the Illuminations Department were not the only things to light up Blackpool that year, for at the Pleasure Beach there was yet another major fire! Flames rising 150ft into the sky engulfed the Big Dipper, causing thousands of pounds worth of damage to the structure, the work of the Fire Brigade being hampered by a strong wind and the inevitable huge crowds, drawn moth-like to the flame.

Above : **Elizabeth I and II tableau 1952, which had a stained glass window design.**

Below: **Patriotic tableaux used to be a common feature of the Illuminations, like this one in 1960.**

Blackpool was a proud place in the summer of 1953 when Blackpool FC won the FA Cup. Naturally, the achievement and team were soon acknowledged in a specially built tableau.

Life in 3D

The Illuminations Department pulled out all the stops for the 1953 display. Spray plastic had again been used for creating three-dimensional shapes, this time a 'Mermaids Retreat' with various forms of sea life. As with the previous year's illuminated cacti, artistic licence had been used to vividly colour the animals. The six mermaids marked the first form of nudity in the Illuminations, unless of course one includes the nightly goings on under the three piers!

New tableaux included a 35ft 3-D 'Sea Monster', 130ft 'Peter Pan in Neverland' and eight 15ft moving nursery rhyme figures with storybook backgrounds. Most impressive of all was a 650ft tableau called 'Merry England', comprising a village, circus procession, big top, fairground and sideshows. Typical of Blackpool it was the largest illuminated tableau in the world! The 450ft pre-war tableau 'Fairy Wedding' was fittingly renamed 'Fairy Coronation', with the whole display completed with thousands of higher wattage lamps, underlining the claim that the Lights were brighter than ever.

This was definitely the age of 3-D. Several cinemas in the town were now being fitted with the latest plastic screens especially designed to accommodate the latest films that were proving highly popular, yet another typical example of Blackpool moving with the times, as it also would soon do with the introduction of Cinemascope on the wide screen.

The 1953 Illuminations were switched on by Lancashire's own George Formby, who after singing 'When I'm Cleaning Windows' and 'Leaning on a Lamp Post' to the 5,000-strong crowd, toured the Lights aboard the illuminated Lifeboat, carrying his little stick of Blackpool Rock no doubt! (Incidentally, in 2004 the Winter Gardens was

The sheer size of the larger tableaux makes it very difficult to build and erect them within the confines of the depot. The two workmen in the foreground are lucky to be working on the 'Fairy Wedding' tableau at ground level, in 1937. Further along, two men have a more precarious position. Behind the 'Fairy Wedding' can be seen the 'Autumn' tableau, complete with harvest scene and Halloween witch. Many other features can be seen stacked up on the bottom right of this picture.

The laburnum trees were still a popular feature in 1954, as can be seen in this view of the gardens between Gynn Square and Cabin.

Possibly one of the most popular and well remembered tableaux ever built was Swan Lake, pictured here in 1954. It included giant rotating swans accompanied by classical music.

the appropriate setting for a celebration of the 100th anniversary of Formby's birth in 1904 by the George Formby Society.)

For the third year, the Illuminations were televised from specially adapted trams travelling from south to north without a northbound tram being in sight to hold up proceedings.

In 1954, the new Swan Lake Ballet tableau had four swans revolving and was accompanied by a Tchaikovsky soundtrack. This played nightly, except for when there was an evening service at the Church of St Stephen on the Cliffs. The vicar complained that the sound from the tableau was audible in the church and would interfere with his services. Another hiccup for this tableau was a plastic ballerina representing Odette actually falling to pieces when rained on! A new ballerina was constructed for 1955.

The pre-war 'Fairy Wedding' tableau was adapted in 1952 and became the 'Fairy Coronation'.

During June 1954 the town's holiday industry was again hit by fire; the first fire almost destroying the Grand Pavilion on South Pier where, had it not been for the gallant efforts of the fire crews, the pier itself may have been destroyed. So serious was the blaze that the tram service along the Promenade was badly affected. A second fire occurred just a few days later on 30th June; this time it was the Tower that was on fire yet again. Fire, which was caused by a spark landing on a tarpaulin, broke out at the 400ft level and proved rather difficult for the fire brigade to extinguish, however they achieved their objective and little damage was done to the structure. Of course, as usual the crowds turned out in their thousands to watch the latest free show in town!

Royals by lamplight

To honour the visit of HM the Queen and HRH the Duke of Edinburgh to Blackpool for a Royal Performance at the Opera House on 13th April 1955, Blackpool staged a special decorative lighting display. This was a dignified display, featuring royal motifs and only two colours – purple and gold – were used in the presentation. The Lights were displayed over about a quarter of a mile of the Royal route from King's Square to the Opera House entrance. A total of about 12,500 lamps were used and approximately 1¹/₂ miles of festoon was erected.

In King's Square, on the traffic island by the Hippodrome Theatre, there was a specially designed 22ft 'Royal Pylon' complete with plaster lions and a fountain with a waterfall effect. Surmounting the column was a three-dimensional floodlit crown. Around the island, were national shields and 'Loyal Greetings' scrolls. The roadway between King's Square and the Opera House was lined by 37 'Crown Pylons', interlinked by purple and gold festoon lighting, each pylon incorporating 180 golden-yellow lamps with a band of purple lamps at the top and bottom. The crowns on top each had 72 golden-yellow lamps and 12 purple lamps. For obvious reasons the display had to be designed to make sure that the Royal route had no overhead live cables. This was the norm for all Royal visits.

For the Illuminations in 1955, the Corporation decided to reintroduce its inter-war scheme of prizes for the best decorative lighting on private properties. There were three classes and three prizes for each class (£50, £30 and £20). The buildings were required to be lit for the entire Illuminations period and observe daily switch on/off times. The prizes on offer seem paltry by today's standards; perhaps that's why the scheme eventually folded.

In 1955 well over 5,000 people saw the switch-on, and on one Saturday in October, British Rail ran 84 special trains in addition to the normal service. Although the missing crowds came back, so did bad weather, when the town was battered during October by the most severe gale in several years. Irreparable damage was caused to the 'Rainbow Arch' at Squires Gate, and £750 of damage was caused to the 'Old Woman In The Shoe' tableau with further damage caused to the Circus tableau, 'Old Mother Hubbard' scene, and the naval tableau. The 12-hour, 70 to 80 mph gale was the costliest ever in a single night. Not only the Lights suffered damage; many properties in the town were also badly affected. (A similar storm in 1957 would be responsible for blowing over one of the twin Ferris wheels on the Pleasure Beach.)

During 1956, the Association of Public Lighting Engineers held its annual conference at the Winter Gardens. To coincide with this, leading manufacturers staged an unlit display of over 100 electric lamp standards of every type and design on the Middle Walk, with other equipment and apparatus on display in a lighting exhibition at the Winter Gardens themselves, where visitors were expected from as far away as Australia, Belgium, Holland, France, India and New Zealand.

'Ali Baba and the Forty Thieves' was one of eight 50ft tableaux from 1955 with a pantomime theme. It was joined by 'Aladdin', 'Alice in Wonderland', 'Snow White', 'Dick Whittington', 'Cinderella', 'Gulliver' and 'The Old Woman in the Shoe'.

The 'Modern Witch' tableau shows a vacuum cleaner being used as a broomstick. Witches have always played a part in Lancashire folklore. This tableau was featured from the 1930s until the 1950s.

Harry Carpenter was also approached to be the Association's new president for that year.

This same year also saw several near disasters in the town. On 29th June Redman's café and shop collapsed into Bank Hey Street as builders were refurbishing the structure. The collapse killed one female pedestrian and injured fifteen others, although it is a miracle that the toll was not higher due to the street being thronged with people at the time. Builders working on the construction of the nearby British Home Stores, along with the emergency services, valiantly dug the victims from the rubble.

Another major incident occurred in December of that year when the Tower ballroom was completely gutted by fire. This fire was so severe and had spread so quickly that at first arson was suspected. Eventually the cause was put down to a smouldering cigarette setting fire to a chair in the office. Rebuilding the ballroom was a major task costing hundreds of thousands of pounds, but the specialist teams that

This 1957 view shows how far the Illuminations display had come on. Illuminated pylons had joined the festoon to create a more complex and extravagant display.

brought the ballroom back to its former glory did such a fantastic job that today no-one could suspect that the Tower complex had come within a whisker of being destroyed completely.

Dispense with the Tableaux indeed!

The Autumn Illuminations in 1957 were a success, especially impressing the American Ambassador, John H Whitney, who in a speech given after he switched the lights on compared the Promenade with Broadway in New York. According to Whitney, Blackpool outshone that famous street, just as it had done in 1879. Nevertheless, not everyone was impressed. Some of the 1000-strong Bispham, Norbreck and Anchorsholme Ratepayers' Association, holding its annual meeting in January 1958, complained that many of the cliffs tableaux were too large and hid residents' and visitors' view of the sea. A petition, signed by about 40 people, successfully asked for the size of tableaux to be reduced. Harry Carpenter stated that the focus that year would be on new and 'outstanding' features rather than 'large' features. (By coincidence, even today some Bispham hoteliers are still complaining about being overlooked).

This criticism was nothing compared to the proposal from a councillor at a meeting of the Illuminations Committee in October. He suggested dispensing with the Bispham tableaux and ending the Lights at the Cabin, adding that the displays were no longer popular, and perhaps approximately £12,000 could be saved by scrapping them. The proposal resulted in a shock 50:50 split, with the chairman refusing to vote.

In 1950, the Palace Building next to the Tower had its own display of illuminated tableaux.

Another serious fire afflicted the South Pier, resulting in damage estimated at over £100,000 at the time. Of course, the holiday crowds were treated to another free show, in fact so often did such fires happen in the resort that one wag writing to the local press suggested they be advertised as an attraction in their own right!

A memorable switch-on night was held in 1959, when Jayne Mansfield did the honours. Arriving at Starr Gate, she boarded the new illuminated tram, the Blackpool Belle, for a tour of the Lights. As she began the journey, a young man aged about 17 started to run alongside. Despite all the crowds on the Promenade, he managed to keep up all the way to Bispham. As the tram approached the terminus, Miss Mansfield asked for the fan to be brought to her. "I want to give him a great big kiss," she said. Arriving at Bispham, the tram stopped, but the man had disappeared into the crowds, not knowing the treat that would have been bestowed upon him. The adoring crowds were unaware that within only a short time this beautiful actress would die in a horrific road accident. Sadly she was never to visit the resort again.

The 1959 Lights had been a huge success for the Transport Department. On one Saturday in

September, they broke all records, taking £7,562 (£150,000 today). By the end of the autumn, 125,759 people had been taken on a tour of the Lights – 27,077 more than in 1958 – possibly due to the fact that illuminated vehicles had been used for tours for the first time.

After 45 years with Blackpool Corporation, Assistant Technical Illuminations Officer George Winkley retired in March 1960. Throughout his time in the Department he had witnessed the blossoming of the Lights into the world famous spectacle they became. Arthur Elliott took on the role at this time, and later in 1974 he was actually appointed director.

As time went by, gas lamps were being systematically phased out; the ornate gas lamp in Highfield Road, near the junction with Lytham Road, puzzled many locals. It gained notoriety by being alight all day and night and many thought it a waste of money. This lamp was not wasting money but was actually one of three that instead of burning coal gas from the mains, acted as safety valves by burning gases from the sewers below the streets. A tall, mock lighthouse structure on the Promenade opposite Manchester Square performs that function today, its light convincing some visitors that it is in fact a real lighthouse.

Following the success of the 650 ft tableau 'Merry England' in 1953, the Illuminations Department felt it was time for a new and larger scene. The 750ft 'Mardi Gras' tableau, built in 1960, depicted a carnival procession and comprised eight floats: Disney Fire Engine, King Carnival, Wedding Cake, Oriental, King Neptune, Pirate Ship, Snow and Ice and Space Age. These were joined by other carnival figures in fancy dress and altogether the tableau consisted of 5,000 lamps. Also new was a 'Magic Story Book' tableau, which at 75ft was only a tenth of the size of Mardi Gras. Remarkably it also consisted of 5,000 lamps – possibly the brightest illuminated tableau ever!

The issue of nudity in illuminated features was raised again in 1960. Dozens of protest letters had been written in 1959 due to the new tableau 'The Birth of Venus'. The mermaids featured on the King Neptune scene provoked another set of complaints. The story was reported in the press as: "Millie the Mermaid and her buxom sisters have already brought a touch of not unwelcome notoriety to the Mardi Gras tableau." The complaints about Millie were answered by a determined

Above left: **Presiding over the switch-on ceremony of 1957 was American Ambassador, John H. Whitney.**

Above right: **Jayne Mansfield throws the switch in 1959.**

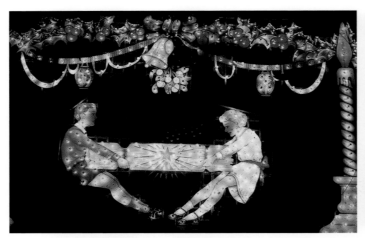

The 'Seasons' tableaux of 1956 depicted different scenes of the time of the year. This one shows a Christmas scene, from the 'Winter' tableau.

With many tableaux being painted, scenes that were illuminated by spotlights enabled artists to create mini-masterpieces on the Promenade. The 'Fantasia' tableau was photographed in 1957.

Illuminations Committee: "That's the way she's staying….without a bra or even a wisp of seaweed across her bosom." There is no record as to whether a certain Mrs Mary Whitehouse was behind the complaints.

Coronation Street's continuing popularity led to the first of three links between Blackpool Illuminations and the northern soap opera. In 1961 Granada TV rearranged filming schedules to allow the cast to board a coach and drive to Blackpool in time for the switch-on. Violet Carson (Ena Sharples) had the honour of pulling the lever. She had lived in Blackpool since 1933, yet she had never seen a switch-on ceremony before, which is rather odd, especially when one considers that for years she worked with Wilfred Pickles. Granada announced that their scriptwriters would be writing her speech as she would be dressed as Ena, whereupon Violet retorted, "I make my own speeches." For the traditional tour of the Illuminations, she stated that she would be removing her hairnet, comb and coat and be herself, refusing to ride in an open tram "dressed like an old hag"! What a woman!

Below left: **In 1953 the topless mermaids of 'Mermaid's Retreat' caused a bit of a stir.**

Below right: **The switch-on ceremony in 1961 with Violet Carson.**

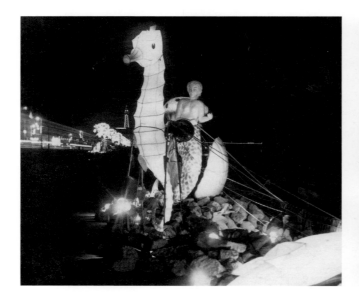

Blackpool transformed   **10**

The 'swinging' sixties of mini-skirts and Mary Quant saw the building of the 'Rocket' illuminated tramcar, the 'Hovertram' the 'Frigate' and the 'Western Train', but also saw the demise of the popular 'Lifeboat' and the 'Gondola', each now considered past its sell by date. This energised and enigmatic era heralded a new age in the history of the Lights, with groundbreaking effects now possible due to the widespread introduction of fibreglass. This innovative and weatherproof material allowed 3-D shapes of any size or design to be fabricated, which could not only be floodlit, but also internally lit for even better effect. Other developments in decorative lighting, such as 'linear light' or 'rope light', led to companies approaching Blackpool Illuminations Department, keen to show off their futuristic designs. One such design was the 'Roto-sphere'; imported from America in 1962, this consisted of sixteen 8ft long projecting fins, each illuminated by double outlined tubing in contrasting colours. It was mounted on a 22ft high tubular mast and its multicoloured effects made it a big hit on the Promenade.

Other innovations in this period included the increased use of transistorised sequence controllers; these in turn led to more imaginative designs for the displays and the ever more complex tableaux, such as the Jungle Life feature. But many of the old stalwarts, such as the now hackneyed and out-of-date Laburnum trees, were still around, though the end was now in sight.

On the entertainment scene the decade saw many changes, with new venues created and other long-standing venues disappearing. Amongst the newcomers were the Lobster Pot group, which not only ran a chain of high-class restaurants in the town, but also had several venues featuring cabaret. The most fashionable of these was the Movenpick Theatre Restaurant, situated in the old Jenkinson's café and bar at Talbot Square, opposite the Town Hall. Here top line artistes played to sophisticated diners in a move that was very 'West End', and which proved quite popular amongst the locals. The Company also ran a ten-pin bowling establishment, complete with theatre restaurant and cabaret bar. This bar saw early appearances of comedian Freddie Starr and many top line pop stars. There were also at least four gambling casinos in the town, including the Castle on North Promenade, and the Winmarith at South Shore to the rear of the Pleasure Beach. Clearly the idea of casinos in

The 'Wild West' section is seen here in 1965. Many themes are repeated at regular intervals in different styles. In 1985 a 'Way out West' tableau was created, again with a cowboy theme.

Jungle Safari in 1964.

The 'Diddy Men' joined Ken Dodd on stage for the 1966 switch-on. The giant stick of rock was a warmly welcomed souvenir of the proceedings.

Blackpool is nothing new, but Blackpool is now aiming for much bigger complexes.

The town still boasted more than twelve cinemas, having lost several over the years due to falling audiences, no doubt due to the advent of television. The same also applied to the live theatres, for during the 60s the Palace Theatre complex was demolished making way for the huge Lewis's store, whilst the Queens Theatre, ex-Feldman's, was also demolished in order to make way for the new C&A store. In a bizarre twist of fate both Lewis's and C&A stores have also now been demolished to make way for other less exotic developments. The Lewis's store was a particular loss to the Illuminations displays as its gigantic ultra-modern honeycomb backlit façade lent a touch of finesse to the scene, whilst the proprietors also gave handsomely to the Lights Fund.

The Beatles were just one of many star turns that appeared during the 1960s. They played the ABC/Hippodrome, which also hosted the evergreen Cliff Richard, Shirley Bassey, Tom Jones and Adam Faith. The Winter Gardens included the Rolling Stones amongst their turns, causing a near riot in the audience of thousands at the Empress Ballroom. The pop group never played there again, but Charlie Barlow and his Beat Boys did; in fact, Charlie, one of the best around, played the venue for 47 years in total. No doubt Ken Dodd, who switched the Lights on in 1966, would have been tickled to hear that, he being a great friend of Charlie. Talking of Charlies, Charlie Cairoli was still packing 'em in at the Tower Circus as usual.

Sir Matt Busby of Manchester United fame switched the 1968 Lights on, but possibly the most innovative switch-on to date was that which occurred when a Warton-built Canberra bomber flew past the Town Hall in 1969, the pilot electronically pulling the switch. (The most unique, however, must surely be the switch-on in 1977, attended by Red Rum, the famous, Southport-based horse; what a star turn he was!)

Without a doubt the 1960s was an era of great change; change which affected every strata of social life in Britain, if not the world. Changes such as the advent of television and cheap continental holidays badly affected Blackpool and other resorts; now the British worker was no longer confined to the shores of these islands, the world was now his oyster. Although Blackpool in particular was still immensely popular, there were subtle changes in the air; these changes soon became apparent to all as the scramble to holiday abroad became ever more prevalent. Not all in tourism recognised the signs, however, and it must be said that collateral damage was done to Blackpool's holiday industry by those who failed to respond to the threats. This situation wasn't helped by the closure of the immense Central Railway Station, which had brought countless millions into the heart of resort. A further blow came about when the huge North Railway Station was demolished and replaced by something a fraction of the size, the station buildings now occupying what had once been an engine shed. Rail services to and from the resort have suffered badly ever since.

Now Blackpool's millions of holidaymakers were increasingly likely to be day-trippers or short stayers, rather than those staying for the usual two weeks. As a consequence there was not the same amount of money flowing into the town. Some businesses began to suffer, but such were the crowds that this affected only a few at the time. Later, when car ownership and travel abroad became even more affordable, the rate of decline escalated, so that by the 1970s, it was becoming evident that Blackpool needed to adapt to the times. At this point in time there were several voices calling for the culling of the Lights, when in actual fact their contribution to the local economy was to become more vital than ever before.

During the 1970s and 1980s, the decline and change in Blackpool's fortunes continued unabated, still often unheeded by some. Several cinemas closed their doors for the last time, with theatre audiences dwindling alarmingly, whilst the larger department stores also began to struggle for survival due to the lack of long stay visitors to the town. Amongst the victims was the huge Co-Op department store in the town centre, which not only closed its doors for business but also resulted in the loss of the little gem of the Jubilee Theatre at roof level. Of course, the usual big fires also took place, with the piers figuring more often than not, whilst the huge RHO Hills department store (later renamed Binns) was completely destroyed by fire, only to be replaced by a smaller development.

To compound all of this, the original Golden Mile was blitzed out of existence. The ramshackle jumble that the visitors knew and loved was destroyed only to be replaced by faceless concrete block-houses containing thousands of slot machines. Much of the flavour and uniqueness had gone forever. Perhaps the only exception of

In 1961 'The Birds and Bees' was one of the first themed sections. It is seen here on the narrowest parts of the Promenade – between Cocker Square and Gynn Square.

Below left: **The 101 Dalmations Tableau in 1961.**
Below right: **A paint job for Pongo. The 101 Dalmations have their final touches applied in 1961.**

A very rare combination in Blackpool – snow and Illuminations during the winter of 1981/82.

The birds of paradise transformed the carriageway into a tropical bird land in 1984. 'Paradise Parade' was a very colourful section with pulsating plumages.

'The Old Woman in the Shoe' tableau, seen here in 1963. Not all tableaux included animation or sophisticated lighting effects. This helped those that did to stand out, and also kept the costs down!

note, which occurred after the blitzkrieg, was the erection of Coral Island on the site of the former (and much missed) Palatine Hotel.

This period also witnessed the destruction of the world famous Derby Baths at North Shore, and the sweeping away of the stunningly beautiful Open Air Baths at South Shore, the latter replaced by the initially unsuccessul Sandcastle Waterworld.

During the 1970s and 1980s, the Illuminations team produced fund raising schemes and ever more imaginative and brighter displays, funded in part by the viewing public who were invited to place cash into the specially erected collection points on the Promenade. Features from the 1950s and 1960s were re-engineered

Animals have featured heavily over the years. New in 1967 the 'Jungle Life' tableau featured internally illuminated fibreglass animals.

The 'Mardi Gras' tableau in 1960 was the first carnival tableaux since the last ill-fated Blackpool Carnival in 1924. The failure of the carnival ensured the survival of the Illuminations.

for a new generation, including the ground-breaking 'Birdcage Walk', which was updated for the 1978 Illuminations. 'Capital Highlights' of 1977 was a display showing views of London, but this led to the question of why Blackpool was promoting other tourist attractions. The designs were changed and, in 1980, the boxes re-emerged as a set of saucy seaside postcards, 'Seaside Chuckles'. The Great British Seaside Holiday was again promoted in the 1979 tableau, 'Holiday Time', and the sights of Blackpool became a feature in 1985 as 'England Entertains',

Again it was easy to see that the Lights were playing an ever more important role in Blackpool's continued success; the summer season was shrinking and undergoing change, whilst the autumn season was now being stretched. At this point in time there were two opposing views around; one school of thought suggesting that the Lights be severely curtailed whilst, on the opposite side of the coin, others were demanding that they be lit all season and also at Christmas. Whatever one's point of view, however, the Lights have always generated debate, as well as generating much welcome cash for the town.

A majority of the town's cinemas had now been lost, either disappearing forever or, as with the Princess Electric Theatre on the Promenade and the ABC/Hippodrome theatre on Church Street, they were converted into nightclubs. Others became snooker halls and the like. Luckily the magnificent Art-Deco Odeon cinema on Dickson Road was saved from destruction, it too being converted into a cabaret theatre called Funny Girls.

Other near casualties included the Winter Gardens complex and the brilliant Grand Theatre on Church Street, with rumours that demolition was planned. Only the fact that the Gardens were subject to a Grade Two listing saved that building,

When the Promenade is wet, as it is here in this picture from 1968, the public always get more than they bargain for as reflections, in effect, double the effect of the display.

The Twin Wheels at the Pleasure Beach in 1964 make a striking illuminated feature.

Astraland 1962.

People and Places 1962.

Fountain Fantasia 1967.

Astraland – a workshop scene 1962.

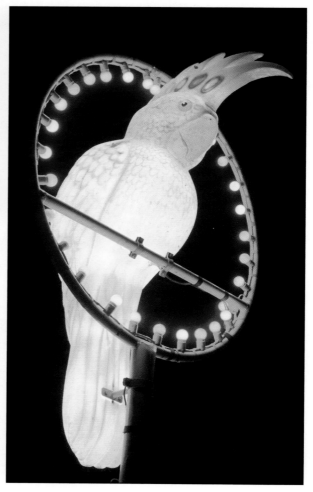

Top: **For the Borough Centenary in 1976, a tableau was built to commemorate the event. 'Bygone Blackpool' depicted scenes of Blackpool in days of old.**

Above: **The Old King Cole tableau of 1978.**

Right: **Showing off the fibreglass to great effect, 'Aviary Art' from 1972 had the all important third dimension, which is always guaranteed to bring a feature to life.**

Above: **Characters from the 'Little Bumbledon' tableau in 1971.**

Above left: **Punch and Judy shows have always been a feature of British seaside towns. The 1979 tableau 'Holiday Time' highlighted many of the things that we love in a traditional British seaside holiday.**

Middle left: **Lewis's Department Store makes a splendid backdrop to the March of Time feature in 1972.**

Bottom left: **The start of the Illuminations used to be signified by a 'welcome' arch, one of which is shown here being erected in 1970. This particular arch survived until 1998, when it was found to be structurally unsound. Nowadays, a pair of illuminated UFOs with the message "Welcome Earthlings" marks the start of the display.**

whilst a massive public outcry and a revenue-raising exercise led by Geoffrey Thompson of the Pleasure Beach saved the incomparable Grand Theatre, which had lately become a bingo hall, bingo perhaps being the one entertainment that had seen any significant growth during the recent past.

By the late 1970s production techniques were well established and features were being made that could better withstand the elements. The 1978 roadway section 'Military Parade' lasted longer than any other Promenade feature of its time, being displayed for the last time in 1987. Almost as durable was the Christmas section 'Festive Follies', also of 1978. The humorous Christmas scenes graced the Promenade until 1982, but then saw further life in Manchester City Centre as part of their Christmas display until 1986. In preparation for the Queen's Silver Jubilee in 1977, a section of giant illuminated crowns was produced for the 1976 Illuminations. 'Queensway' was a very colourful section and the crowns were displayed until 1985 when, in their last year, they were interspersed with the soldiers of 'Military Parade' to create a Royal route on the Promenade. The Juggling Clowns of the 1930s were the inspiration for the 1979 section 'Clowning'. This time the display was more daring, with the clowns juggling across the road to each other as well as firing water pistols at each other. On display until 1983, the clowns were sold on and some are still on display, albeit repainted, at both Blackpool Pleasure Beach and Great Yarmouth Pleasure Beach, now over 25 years since their construction!

The 1980s also saw the continued mix of traditional features and new innovations. The decade saw features representing most of the times of the year including 'Valentine Nights' (1986), 'Easter Time' (1982), 'Halloween' (1981) and 'Christmas Festivities' (1984). Animals also featured highly as these are always popular with children. Representing most of the animal kingdom were 'Fishy Flirtations' (1980), 'Butterfly Boulevard', 'Dinosaur Days' and 'Down On The Farm' (all 1981) and the birds of 'Paradise Parade' (1984). Most other animals had been covered in the 1970s 'Noah's Ark' tableau and 'Pets Parade' section. The only notable exceptions were creepy crawlies who hadn't been a feature since 1961 in the guise of 'The Birds and The Bees'. This was later rectified in the 1990s with the 'Slugs 'n' Bugs' and 'Insect Grotto' features.

For the 50th Illuminations in 1982, fibre optics and lasers were introduced. The 'Fibre optic tab' as it was known used glass optics and a series of individual colour changers, primitive by today's standards but well ahead of its time in 1982. However traditional construction methods and materials were still being used elsewhere. As well as gears and motors, pneumatics were introduced to control movement of the 3-D fibreglass features. The biggest problem with the pneumatics was they used to suffer at the hands of condensed water within the narrow bore pipes; it was a nightly job to drain them. Failure to do this would result in static displays. Pneumatics were, however, used to good effect on the very popular 1985 'Way out West' tableau. Other particularly well received tableaux were the 1987 'Candyland' town, made of sweets, and the 1986 'Tales of Beatrix Potter'. 'Teddy Bears' Picnic' first appeared in 1984 and went on for a further 20 years service, although highly condensed from the original scene.

Staff holidays gave inspiration for new features, including the casino signs of 'Vegas Lites' in 1982. Arthur Elliot was actually dispatched to Las Vegas by the Local Authority to do the research. The Orient had been realised in lights in the 1950s and 1970s, with features called 'Oriental Avenue'. The 1980s saw 'Eastlight' (1981), decorated lanterns called 'Orientalites' in 1985 and a set of Geisha Girls in 1987. This particular roadway section caused much humour as problems were experienced with the girls' heads that were designed to rotate 180 degrees from left to right.

In 1990, a new section called 'Blackpool Magic' was erected between Gynn Square and Cabin. The magicians' hands all had something appearing out of them, or playing cards being fanned.

The 'Blackpool Magic' hand karate-chopped this car in 1990. At first the bemused owner thought it was a hidden camera television stunt. The car was a write-off. (Photograph: Bill Johnson)

Some heads got stuck facing backwards (still rotating 180 degrees!) whilst others were more sinister, continually rotating through 360 degrees!

Also in 1987 a massive and highly complex cutting edge tableau was introduced, 'Magic Lites'. It allowed a digital graphic effect created by thousands of individually wired lamps to create multiple effects, such as sailing boats moving across the display. Programming took hours, but it was a genuine forerunner to the modern Digital LED displays, which are, of course, now much more common. The Illuminations Department could produce such items as it employed the services of a very talented electronics designer, the late Roger Eastmead, who developed electronic football scoring signs, including the first ever one at Maine Road Manchester.

In 1989, a roadway section of giant lightbulb people was built. 'Lamp Lighters' featured, amongst others, Mr and Mrs Noah (Ark Lamps), 'Sally' Sun Lamp, Headmaster 'Hector' Head Lamp, and Policeman 'Bobby' Blue Lamp. One of the designs was for Larry Lamp, whom it was suggested should become the official mascot of the Illuminations. Badges, mugs, cuddly toys and stationary sets were produced and Larry was later sited at Starr Gate to welcome visitors. Unfortunately, Larry didn't catch on and the 'Lamp Lighters' were withdrawn after the 1995 Illuminations.

In 1989 some tableaux were contracted out, being made away from Rigby Road, as was the political flavour of the time. These were 'Real Ghostbusters' and 'Santa's Workshop'. The experiment was only a limited success, aspects of them proved problematical and the Illuminations Department found itself making large scale modifications to them subsequently. Since then the Department has generally built items in-house, unless economics, skills and time combined to make outsourcing a practicable option.

As the 1980s became the 1990s there was magic in the air.

A touch of Blackpool Magic

The 1990s commenced with a flurry of exiting new features. In 1990 the Illuminations Department created one of its most complex and expensive road-sections to date. Called 'Blackpool Magic', it featured giant magicians that literally did illusions in front of onlookers. A card magically appeared out of a hand and hats, rabbits and cards flew magically across the road. The section demanded much of the Illuminations Department and was produced in great haste. It incorporated mechanical motion systems and complex electronics. Current Illuminations

With the exception of the Tower, the 'Big One' rollercoaster is the biggest structure to be illuminated in Blackpool. It is seen here in 1994. (Chris Parker)

An avenue of colour and splendour. The many effects have made this 1998 feature a firm favourite. As well as the aliens' revolving heads, each UFO has a pulsating jet flow and 'shoots' rapid-fire jets of light at other UFOs on diagonally opposite poles. (Chris Parker)

The Illuminations Department excelled themselves in 2002 with this, the 'Fire and Water' tableau. Not only did it include running water, but also the world's first installation of outdoor LED luminaries, called 'Chromascape™'.
(Andrew Hazlehurst)

Manager Richard Ryan recalls: "It was a total nightmare; we kept changing the specification on what we wanted it to do. Eric Bartoszek, the fitter doing the mechanics on the job, and I spent our August Bank Holiday on site at Rigby Road testing and finishing it off!"

Eventually the section proved to be a great success after yet further modification in its second year. Richard added: "The problem is we never get time to prototype as thoroughly as we know we should. It's much better today than it was then, but frankly we frequently went in on a wing and a prayer with newer more complex items. These days we do much more R&D but you can always do more."

In the same year as Blackpool Magic it was agreed to put something new on Gynn Roundabout, so after some debate an electronically operated 'Fountain' was agreed.

"This was as bad as the Magic section for me," recalls Richard Ryan. "It was my first full year in charge of new features and it had reached March and I had not done a thing with Graham's (the Designer) concept sketch for the fountain: a three tiered 3D shape some 40 ft tall. I literally did this design on holiday on the Norfolk Broads in late March on the proverbial 'fag packet'. I knew what I wanted it to do but basically completely underestimated the complexities. I assumed it would somehow just come together."

It got finished just on time and worked as a design but the 110 Volt festoon deployed soon exploded (literally) and the following year it was all replaced free of charge by the manufacturer and 12 Volt systems were used.

Through the 1990s many exiting and innovative items were produced. 1993 saw 'Yule Lights', a section that had no pole feature as such and consisted of galvanised steel meshes to which large amounts of 'non-neon' rope-lighting was attached. The section was major departure and a serious engineering challenge.

"I was petrified we would pull down the street-lighting poles," said Richard. "I had a mechanical engineering colleague in and together we worked out it would only work if we let it sag by about 2 ft across the road. I did a memo to Frank Hilton saying we absolutely must let it sag. Luckily Frank had the courage to go for it and the section was a great success."

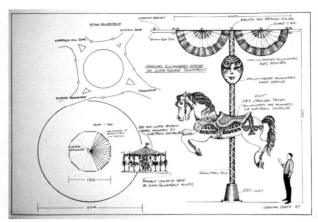

Top left: **The horses for the Carousel at Gynn Square were initially carved in polystyrene. In this view from 1997, you can see the definition for most of the horse has been completed.**
(Andrew Hazlehurst)

Top right: **Original design for the Carousel.**

Bottom left: **Illuminations Designer Graham Ogden at his desk in Rigby Road.**

Bottom right: **The finished Carousel, pictured at Gynn Square in 1999. It has become a familiar sight and is the only Illuminations feature that remains in place throughout the year.**
(Andrew Hazlehurst)

In 1994, James Scott Ltd of Preston was given the contract of upgrading the Promenade infrastructure for the tramway and Illuminations. Totalling £8.88 million, the project comprised the tramway (£4.12m), street lighting (£1.32m) and Illuminations (£3.44m). For the tramway, overhead wiring and traction poles were replaced, with every street lighting column also replaced and evenly spaced in facing pairs approximately 30 metres apart. Supply pillars and all associated electrical cabling were included, whilst existing substations were refurbished with new substations built at Gynn Square, Princess Parade and adjacent to the Pleasure Beach.

All the substations were now connected via fibre optic cable to a computer at the Rigby Road depot. In conjunction with this, a new Supervisory Control and Data Acquisition control system was fitted, allowing the automated switch-on of sections of the Illuminations. Prior to this, each evening twelve men had the job of manually switching on the sections from junction boxes.

A massive rebuilding and strengthening programme, starting with the sea wall at South Shore, has led to the possible permanent loss of tableaux between Starr Gate and the Pleasure Beach, where a totally redesigned Promenade now features permanent works of art of varying popularity, the most striking of which is the giant illuminated 'glitterball', said to be the biggest in the world. Typical Blackpool extravaganza that!

In 1994 Blackpool celebrated with 'Festival 94', a celebration of both the Tower's centenary and the launch of the Pleasure Beach's amazing Big One ride, the tallest and fastest roller coaster in the world. The Illuminations Department produced a spectacular series of grand illuminated canopies as part of this activity.

The Gynn Fountain was retired in 1997 and the spectacular Carousel was installed in its place. Costing £100,000, it is the only illumination to remain on site all year round. Asked why this was the case, Richard Ryan said: "It's just too large to store; we are always struggling for storage space so we leave it out as much as we can get away with!"

Major items were designed and operated to celebrate the 2000 Millennium. In the 1999 season, two road-sections were designed ('Party Poppers' and 'Millennium Discs' – the latter with removable '2000' signs on top allowing re use in future years!) and the show was operated outside its traditional nine-week period. The display ran its usual season then sections of it remained up. Some items were added and re-erected to be relit in late November for the run up to the New Year. From Pleasure Beach to Gynn Square was illuminated each night including the Millennium night itself.

Shining a light on the future

Despite the changes in the public's tastes and fashions – changes which have resulted in many seaside resorts now being almost on their deathbed – Blackpool has been very resilient. It remains Europe's most popular resort destination, almost certainly as a result of the town's continued innovation and regular investment. The Illuminations, along with the Pleasure Beach, have been singled out as one of the town's main strengths in the Northwest Development Agency's 'A New Vision for Northwest Coastal Resorts' (2003). The Illuminations now draw more than 3.5 million visitors to the town every year.

The Illuminations cost around £2.4 million a year to stage (2003 figures) and Blackpool Council still stands the vast majority of this cost, approximately £1.7 million annually (2003). There is no legal requirement for the Council to fund the Illuminations as its it technically a 'non-statutory service' (statutory services being waste disposal, planning, etc). However Blackpool Council continues to fund the Illuminations as it believes in the effectiveness of the display as an economic stimulator, especially to the critically important tourism sector.

In 2002/3 the Council carried out a detailed review and audit, included in which was a cost/benefit analysis. Independently audited research indicated an annual spend in Blackpool's economy of £79 million directly associated with people who came "just to see the lights". Further to this it calculated an economic benefit to Blackpool due to the extension of the season afforded by the Illuminations to be in excess of £279 million.

In effect the Council is investing in an attraction that brings in 100 times its outgoing in terms of business activity. Despite this, the Illuminations is always a political issue and its funding will always be dependent on new developments and its continued success.

Funding from businesses within Blackpool continues to be an important source of revenue, There is a voluntary business collection whereby funds collected only go to the Illuminations service, not other Council departments. The same can be said of the Promenade collection (voluntary donations collected directly from those viewing the display at two positions on the Promenade), which annually inputs over £130,000 to the costs of staging the event.

Sponsorship of sections or tableaux and works carried out for third parties by the Illuminations Department remain the other methods of revenue generation.

The Golden Mile seen in the early 1960s. The illuminated pylons preceded the themed sections that can now be seen on the Promenade.

The 'Haunted Hotel' includes DVD projection as part of its arsenal of effects.

One of the most dazzling Promenade sections ever, 'Diamond Lights', was built to commemorate the 60th Diamond Illuminations in 1992.

To infinity and beyond

One always needs to be very careful when predicting the future, but it is probably a fair bet that the Illuminations will continue to evolve as a spectacle. Public taste and visitor expectations are rapidly changing and people expect to be enthralled year after year. Visitors regularly travel the world now and many set high benchmarks for quality and scale.

The Blackpool Illuminations is a curiously complex mix of old and new – comfort and modernity. It thrives on its history and yet seeks new challenges every year. If one asks visitors what their favourite items are the answers can be surprising. They vary from super complex highly technical tableaux to the simplicity of the nursery rhymes.

In 2003, the feasibility of operating a large mile-wide laser show right across the piers was evaluated involving the world's first white light 40 Watt laser. Technically it was seen as deliverable. Work on the project is ongoing, as it is on a myriad of projects. LED based technologies are also being explored further.

It is envisaged that modern control equipment will enable the street-lighting to be coordinated within the overall spectacle and areas could be dulled down or brightened up to suit moods and themes.

The 2003 'New Horizons' Masterplan is a vision for 21st Century Blackpool. The Masterplan – drawn up by consultants for Blackpool Council – sees the Illuminations as central to marking Blackpool out from the crowd as a "resort of light". The idea is to complement the existing Illuminations display with year-round illumination schemes for prominent buildings, parks and open spaces in the town. The Masterplan also suggests an extended events programme, featuring "a spectacular array of hi-tech, state-of-the-art light shows".

The Masterplan also advocates the use of new, cutting-edge technology to create spectacular effects:

> "Searchlights and lasers could be 'bounced' from the piers to major landmarks like the Tower and the Pleasure Beach – injecting movement and vitality into the

The 'new' Big Wheel on Central Pier, seen here in 1994, is not as large as the original at the Winter Gardens, but it still gives great views from the top.

night sky. Computer animated light shows could be used to create images that would dance in the air like illuminated holograms – a far more dramatic effect than the more common technique of projecting images on to flat screens. The new-look Blackpool could also feature 'media canopies' similar to those used in Las Vegas' Fremont Street. These covered walkways and canopies play music as light displays are projected onto them, turning ordinary streets into free, outdoor entertainment venues."

As part of the Masterplan, external lighting professionals will be invited to give opinions and offer alternative perspectives and possibly schemes. A lighting strategy for Blackpool will become formalised and Illuminations will form an integral part of that process.

Blackpool's tourism advisor Peter Moore believes that the Blackpool Illuminations are one part of Blackpool's heritage that deserves a continuing, central role in the future. He said:

"Illumination provides Blackpool with a special opportunity to create a unique sense of theatre, and to delight and surprise its visitors. The transformation of the current Illuminations into a successful 21st century spectacle will require careful planning, enormous imagination and great technical skill."

Change is a constant and the Illuminations Department is set fair to be critically and positively involved in that change. Asked what he saw as the future of the Illuminations, Richard Ryan speculated:

"It will clearly become more efficient (electrically). I envisage a higher use of LEDS, better overall controllability and laser light. I would like to see more shows or special events within it. Interactivity will increase and I think most critically we will need to sort out the issues of transportation and how the show is actually viewed by our visitors, as this is the aspect of the experience that gets the main criticism. I am confident that Blackpool has the talent to sort these issues out and deliver this ever-improving visitor experience and the display will keep people returning to Blackpool and its many attractions for many years to come."

From humble beginnings – from lamp to laser – the story of the Blackpool Illuminations is far from over.

The New Horizons Masterplan of 2003 presents a vision for the Blackpool of the 21st century, a vision that is already being implemented in phases. The Illuminations are a major part of this Masterplan.

Meanwhile, back at the depot

11

The Illuminations are housed in a large council depot on Blackpool's Rigby Road, less than one mile from the Promenade and sandwiched between a waste refuse storage facility and a donkey stable. Within the Depot the joke is that "it's easy to find us in the summer – follow your nose!"

The formation of a dedicated Illuminations Department in 1936 cemented Blackpool's commitment to the idea of presenting an annual display. For the first formal Illuminations in 1912, the display in Princess Parade was created using strings of lights, dubbed 'festoon'. The advantage of festoon is the way it can be strung from pole to pole, creating a very simple effect, as it still does today. From festoon came the idea to decorate buildings, columns and arches by lining them in strings of lights, thus highlighting their architectural design to the full.

To further add variety on the Promenade, small tableaux were created. Simple designs of butterflies were constructed on wire frames and hung from poles. When lit up, the outline of the wings and body created one of the first specially designed features. By 1928, artists were employed to paint different pictures on plywood. These were then illuminated either by floodlight, or by lamps poking through the design. To accentuate the colour of these early tableaux, lamps were dipped in paint or sprayed to give the correct colour.

The success of the tableaux on the Promenade, and the limited number of tableaux installed on the cliffs at Bispham in 1930, led to an ambitious move in 1932, when the decision was made to host a major display of tableaux on the cliffs between Cabin and Bispham. Movement was given to these early tableaux by connecting a motor to a rotating drum fitted with electrical contacts. As the drum rotated, different circuits became live, lighting different parts of the tableau as it went. This simple device allowed such things as the mouse to run up the clock on the Hickory Dickory Dock tableau, the Juggling Clowns to juggle, Cinderella's coach to 'move' and electric fireworks to go off on the 'November 5th' tableau. The use of motors, gears and levers also gave rise to motion in the displays and, by placing smaller features in front of larger backdrops, a 3-D feel was created. Yet it wasn't until the 1950s that true 3-D could be realised.

Experiments with plastics in 1950 saw the creation of floral designs for the 'Concours des Fleurs' section, which also featured on the Town Hall. Birdcage Walk in

Sited on Rigby Road, the Illuminations Depot is where all features are built and stored.

(Andrew Hazlehurst)

Above left: **The 'Summer' tableau of the 1930s was almost complete when this picture was taken. The finishing touches are being applied.**

Above right: **When Blackpool got the 'all clear' in 1949, work began on assembling as much of the 1939 display as possible. Kept in store for ten years, some of the features were cannibalised for the war effort. However, the infamous clowns, once displayed on the Town Hall, were one feature to survive, and helped re-launch the annual spectacle to an eager public.**

Right: **Just as in the famous song, these ladies were 'forever blowing bubbles'. Well, at least until their retirement! The layout of the lamp sockets has been carefully planned to match the outline of the feature design. For practical reasons, the lamps were fitted once the tableau had been erected on the cliffs. This picture shows them being fitted inside the depot in 1929, probably for testing purposes.**

1951 consisted of 10 to 15 feet high parrots, parakeets, budgerigars, lovebirds and canaries in metal cages. These were constructed by applying a sprayed-on plastic called Chrysaline to a wire frame, a process similar to that used by the Royal Navy when 'mothballing' warships. This technique was further used for the cacti of 'Arizona Avenue' and the sea creatures of 'Mermaids' Retreat'. Plastic was also used on the tableaux. Translucent plastic sheet panels were painted and attached to boxes that were lit internally. This process, using acrylic sheets, is still used today!

The introduction of fibreglass was a milestone in the construction of features. It could be made into every conceivable shape, spray-painted and internally lit. The use of moulds allowed the simple mass production of features too. Even after 30 years, fibreglass still had a major part to play in the Illuminations.

A more recent addition has been the use of vacuum formed plastics. Once a mould has been made, the shapes can be produced very quickly at a fraction of the

As features become weather beaten, re-sprays and rewires take place to ensure reliability and attractiveness for the following year's display. This figure, from the 1986 Harlequinade display, has just received a wash and brush-up.

Above left: **Fibreglass alien heads sit patiently in the Depot, waiting to be painted in 1998.**
(Andrew Hazlehurst)

Above right: **Open Day has been a feature of the Illuminations Depot for many years. It allows press and public alike to inspect new features and get a behind-the-scenes look at how the Illuminations are constructed. A small selection of 'Butterfly Boulevard' is shown being displayed in 1981.**

Left: **A coat of emulsion is added to protect the polystyrene from the fibreglass. One of the 'Thomas the Tank Engine' features is treated here in 1986.**

Above left: **A stencil is used to cut out the plywood backboard.**

Above right: **The resulting feature ... Arc (or should that be 'Ark'?) lamps return to the Promenade in 1989 in the guide of Mr and Mrs Noah!**

(Andrew Hazlehurst)

time taken to produce fibreglass models. Another advantage is that vacuum formed shapes can be painted on the inside, thus protecting the paintwork from the weather and from other damage.

The arrival of microchip technology allowed the withdrawal of the outdated and potentially lethal rotating drums used to control animation. Being able to programme and re-programme features allows different effects to be tested before being finalised. Until 2003 these were based on 'EEprom' systems. However, these have now been superseded by more modern 'PIC' technology. This allows a reduced component count on boards making electronic control processes cheaper, more flexible and simpler.

Hand-operated searchlights have also given way to microprocessor controlled searchlights and lasers. Interactive features have been introduced, as well as computer games which are projected onto large screens. Sony™ Eyetoy systems have also been added following a tie up with the Japanese computer giant.

It's a design thing

With a set budget, short timescales and limited manpower, the Illuminations Designer has to balance designs very carefully. One of the constraints is making sure that all of the craftsmen; carpenters, electricians, metalworkers, carvers, mould makers and painters who work at the Depot have sufficient work to last the year. Former Illuminations Directors Harry Carpenter and Arthur Elliott always carried notebooks in which to jot down ideas for features. At the time of writing many of the ideas were coming from one man, designer Graham Ogden.

A student of London's Goldsmiths School of Art, Graham started at the Illuminations Department in 1973 as a labourer (despite having a Degree in Art and Design!) His first job was washing down fibreglass casts. After two years as a Junior Artist, he progressed onto Senior Artist and later Developmental Artist. In 1987 he took on the position of Illuminations Designer. After more than 30 years at the Depot, Graham is enjoying it as much as ever:

"It's not a real job," he said. "It's immensely creative and I really do feel privileged to be doing what I do for my living."

To retain popularity, there must be frequent changes and new features every year. Harry Carpenter highlighted the main elements of design as "interest, attraction, design, illumination, artistry and construction". New features have to appeal to all ages and impress the public, creating talking points. Popular themes need to be included and displays should be attractive by day as well as by night. Lighting techniques should be considered and presentations should be pleasing and colourful. Above all, construction needs to take place with public safety in mind and features have to be durable in all weathers.

"Ideas come from everywhere I suppose," said Graham, "but for the past few years, I've been getting inspiration from my holidays. Last year was Hawaii, so this year's theme (2004) is an Aloha and Hula Paradise."

Graham works in a department headed by Illuminations Manager, Richard Ryan, whose job it is to deliver everything required for the Illuminations from within the confines of the Depot. As Richard Ryan explains, the Depot complex is a mass of conflicting design styles:

"The Depot is assembled from buildings of different eras. In 1936 the basic Rigby Road facility was set up from buildings that had housed the Blackpool Corporation's stables. We used to share the building with the Council's street lighting service, but in 1989 this was privatised and the Depot now houses just the Illuminations team. There are three large, high roofed, heated production sheds, two large unheated storage sheds and an assortment of trade shops (Fibreglass, Art , Spraying, Fitting, Electrical, Festoon, Electronics, 'High Tech' and paint shops). The 'new shed' storage facility is so called as it is only 20 years old!

"Over time the Depot has been added to and improved, but the ad-hoc nature of this has lead to certain production difficulties. For example, steel fitting work is done in an area completely divorced from fibreglass, when ideally they belong side by side.

Left: **When working with polystyrene, the resulting shapes (in this case Muppets) must be covered in plaster. Doing the honours ,in this picture from 1978, is Graham Ogden, who is now Illuminations Designer.**

Right: **Space within the Depot is very limited. As well as storing the features, all new features are built there too. There are no posh studios for these painters! A laburnum tree can be seen here in 1938, together with an illuminated arch, stacked tableaux and other features.**

"To produce the complexity of Illuminations the Department produces, specialised equipment is required. The Depot boasts fully functioning welding bays, fabricating workshops with lathes, drills and saws, spray booths, electronic workshops and RCD protected electrical supplies. All this is expensive to maintain and operate and it is true to say the equipment is in generally better condition than the basic infrastructure of the Depot itself.

As Graham Ogden explains, new technology arrives all the time:

"There has been a huge amount of change over the years, but the biggest change in my job came in 2001 when the Department bought me a computer. Since that day I have not touched traditional artist tools, like paint and brushes."

Behind The Magic – A Year In The Making

Apart from the forced breaks due to the wars, the design, production, erection, display and dismantling of the Illuminations has been a never-ending process. Being a repetitive cycle, the plans and designs for the autumn Illuminations are actually initiated 18 months prior to erection and display.

The first visible signs of the Illuminations on the Promenade occur in April. Every pole is numbered and the whole Promenade is divided into approximately 20 sections. Most sections are 12 pole pairs in length. To add variety to the display the festoon is strung in different pre-determined patterns and often in colours to complement the sections. The cliffs tableaux are also planned down to the last pole.

Armed with their detailed plans, the engineers then emerge onto the Promenade and bring the sections out for erection. The roadway features are erected first, usually starting on the South Promenade and working north. Erection of the features causes some disruption, as at least three vehicles are required at one time – one to carry the features, a crane to hoist the feature and place it in the required position and a third vehicle with the engineer in an elevated 'bucket' to fasten the feature to the pole. Between Central and North Piers, adjacent to the town centre, the Illuminations are assembled outside normal working hours – requiring night time working – as the Promenade is extremely busy in this area. The narrow roadway between Cocker Square and Gynn Square is another section where late night erection is required.

The ornate lamp holders on the Promenade took several men to hoist them into position. They were a feature from 1893 until the modernisation programme of the 1950s. One can be seen here being fitted near to the Tower.

Left: **Work in progress for the 'Birds and Bees' Promenade section for the 1938 display.**

Right: **The corrosive nature of the weather requires the regular painting of the lampposts on the Promenade. You cannot envy these two men, seen here in 1965, when you think how many poles there are along five miles of Promenade!**

Timed to coincide with the peak summer period, the erection of roadway features is completed by July. By this time the steel poles will have been fitted on the cliffs, so that attention can be given to the tableaux. The back scenes of each tableau are loaded in sections onto vehicles in the depot and transported to the cliffs for attachment to the poles. The front figures follow later and the completed tableaux are then connected to the electrical supply.

During the 1930s, tableaux had to be manually fitted without the aid of a hydraulic crane. After the poles had been sited, timber was attached for the tableaux to be strapped to. These would then be manually lifted and fastened to the timber. Today's techniques are much more efficient and allow larger and heavier features to be erected. A camouflaged concrete road, for example, has been fitted along the cliffs to prevent heavy lorries getting stuck in mud or churning up the grass.

From June, the new features are fitted on the Promenade as soon as they are completed. New tableaux are transported to the cliffs so that the whole display can be connected and tested by the last week in August.

A few days prior to the official switch-on, the whole Illuminations are switched on for a practice run, allowing a preview for holidaymakers and press. Even after the switch-on ceremony there isn't time to rest. Way back in June, plans were already being prepared for the new features for next year. Contracts with sponsors have to

One of the lorries used by the council to maintain and erect the features in the 1950s.

be in place early enough to give the designer time to design the roadway feature or tableau to the clients' specifications. By September, the ideas have been finalised, engineers consulted about construction and building plans drawn up. Whilst the Depot is relatively empty in September and October, it is an ideal time to start on the new features.

All too quickly the 66 nights of the Illuminations pass, and the long but well planned dismantling programme is executed. The tableaux, which are particularly exposed to the weather, are dismantled first. Features are checked, electrically and mechanically, repairs and cleaning carried out, then they are stored in the Depot ready for the

Above: **Many themes have been repeated over the years. Christmas sections and miniature tableaux have an added bonus, as they can be re-erected in the town centre for the Christmas period.**

following year. The aim is to have every feature stored in the depot by Christmas. The only exceptions are the items that form the Christmas display in the town centre. These are erected in September and October and supplemented by any Christmas themed pole features after being dismantled from display on the Promenade. In January the Christmas display is dismantled, but work at the Depot doesn't end there, continuing behind closed doors until April comes around again.

Right: **With the Illuminations over for another year, all features and tableaux have to be dismantled and brought back to the depot for testing and storage.**

Decorated tramcars

12

The first trams to be specially illuminated were seen on 22nd June 1897. Five cars were decorated with patriotic slogans to celebrate Queen Victoria's Diamond Jubilee. Power for these illuminations was supplied by onboard batteries.

The Coronation of King Edward VII in 1902 was celebrated with 25 specially illuminated trams, decked out in red, white and blue lamps. In 1911, the Coronation of King George V and Queen Mary was celebrated with three tramcars bedecked with flags and lights. The opening of the new Promenade in 1905 saw eight cars illuminated.

In 1912, Princess Parade was opened and the first formal Illuminations display took place. This ceremony saw another tramcar being illuminated in celebration. New double deck 'De Luxe' 68 was decorated with 3,000 lamps and messages welcoming Princess Louise. These were changed to 'Long Live Our King and Queen In Health and Happiness' for the Royal visit of 1913. Car 68 was seen illuminated once more in 1914, but the not again until 1925 when the Illuminations returned to the Promenade. From 1925, until its withdrawal after the Illuminations of 1936, it carried slogans welcoming visitors and the Blackpool motto, 'Progress'.

Although a common sight in modern Illuminations displays, Blackpool's first specially built feature tram was not built with the Illuminations in mind. In order to raise funds for the war effort, a tram was built to resemble a tank. Numbered 88 and named 'Albert', it lasted only a short time before being converted back to a works car.

The re-introduction of the Illuminations in 1925 saw the first purpose-built illuminated feature car. Former service car, Marton Box 28, was stripped down and a new body constructed in the style of a Venetian gondola. Painted white with a red band and gold finery, the Gondola also had a pagoda style canopy with ornate scrollwork. It didn't, however, include a door for the crew to board! Access was gained via a stepladder and apart from the crew only specially invited guests rode on board. For the 1925 season the crew were dressed as gondoliers and a small orchestra played. The Gondola continued in service until the 1960s.

Car 3 was illuminated in 1905 for the opening of the new Promenade.
(Blackpool Transport)

After the success of the Gondola and the 1925 Illuminations, plans were made for the 1926 Lights to be bigger and better. An illuminated lifeboat was constructed using the remains of Marton Box car 40. It was named 'Jubilee' to coincide with the 50th Anniversary of Blackpool's incorporation as a borough. Authentically painted in RNLI colours, the Lifeboat also had a 'sail' of lights that could be turned to face the direction of travel. Like the Gondola, it only carried invited guests, one of whom was the Duke of Kent, who visited on 21st October 1926.

The Lifeboat was adapted for use as a fare-paying tram in 1959 with folding steps and seats for 20 passengers fitted. However, after 35 years in service it was withdrawn after the Illuminations of 1961.

The 'Gondola' swept gracefully down the Promenade from 1925. Even to this day, the illuminated feature cars operate "subject to the weather".

It wasn't until 1933 that another feature car graced the Promenade. Works Car 2 was quickly rebuilt to resemble Anne Hathaway's rustic thatched cottage and garden. The cottage was built complete with genuine thatched roof, a feature that – considering Blackpool's autumn climate – probably contributed to its very limited use before being scrapped two years later. The crew reluctantly had to dress in rustic smocks to match the theme of the tram.

For the 1937 Illuminations it was decided to replace De Luxe Car 68 with a feature car built as futuristic tram – from the year 2937 to be exact. The streamlined body had false saloon windows and a door in the centre for the driver to board. Its shape soon got it the nickname 'Cottage Loaf'. In 1938, the 'Progress' tram was redecorated to highlight air raid precautions and following the outbreak of war was used for various Government wartime initiatives, ending the War as a star attraction at the VE and VJ day celebrations.

Rebuilt in 1949 to be similar to a streamlined double decker, the Progress car featured a false top deck and windows with silhouettes of people in them. The word 'Progress' adorned both ends, whilst the sides had slogans welcoming visitors, as well as designs representing Blackpool Tower and a town crier. Unfortunately, the decision to build a tableau of the Mayflower crossing the Atlantic Ocean on the side in 1958 resulted in damage to the framework and the tram was soon withdrawn and scrapped.

In 1959, it was decided to illuminate two service cars by covering them in lamps fitted around windows and the panels. Standard Cars 158 and 159

The open 'Toastrack' trams, some of which are seen here in 1926, were very popular for tours. Strings of lights were added as an extra feature during the Illuminations. As well as being decorative, they also helped the conductor to collect fares after dark!

Above: **New in 1926, the 'Lifeboat' was another popular tram on the Promenade. The sail could be turned to face the direction of travel.**

Left: **The 'Progress car' in its pre-war guise of futuristic tram, seen here in 1937. The writing around the clock face says "progress 2937" to reflect a tram 1,000 years into the future. Blackpool's coat of arms is proudly displayed on the sides.**

Top: **The crew shown here were taking no chances! The Progress tram advertises air-raid precautions in 1938. (Blackpool Transport)**

Middle: **Car 68 made a huge impression on the people who saw it on the Promenade. Blackpool's motto, 'Progress', was illuminated proudly on its ends. It is seen here in the 1920s. (Andrew Hazlehurst Collection)**

Bottom: **After the war, the 'Progress car' was rebuilt as a double-decker, although it didn't have an upper deck, nor carry passengers. It ran from 1949 until 1958.**

also had stars fitted on the ends and painted adverts on the sides promoting the Illuminations. The pair operated from 1959 to 1966. Number 158 was scrapped, but 159 is now preserved, minus its illuminations, at the East Anglia Transport Museum near Lowestoft.

The Standards were not the only new illuminated features in 1959. Number 163 was rebuilt as a Mississippi paddle steamer. Named the 'Blackpool Belle' and numbered 731, it carried 32 passengers on its lower decks and played recorded music on the Promenade. In 1967 it carried advertisements for the first time, for Premium Bonds. From 1968, until its withdrawal in 1978, Haig Whisky was advertised.

The space race gave the inspiration for the next feature car. By far the most unusual tram in the fleet, the 'Rocket', was built in 1961 from Pantograph 168 with a saloon at an angle of 20°. A false cockpit in front of the passengers contained two astronauts, both spare waxworks from Tussauds. The driver's cab was sited separately underneath. Whilst the Soviet Union had the Sputnik, Blackpool had Tramnik One, a name carried on the front, until replaced by adverts in 1968. Numbered 732, the Rocket was withdrawn after the Illuminations of 1999.

The most popular of all illuminated feature cars, the 'Western Train', was built in 1962 and is the only illuminated twin-car. The locomotive was built from Railcoach 209 and the trailer from a minimally adapted Pantograph 174, the original design for which was suitable for conversion. Based on a design of a Santa Fe train, it originally had the ability to make smoke. Unfortunately the local weather had the ability to blow the smoke directly in the faces of queuing passengers! Originally sponsored by ABC Television, Western Train 733/734 later carried adverts for Stardrops/Zoflora, Woolworths and, since 1979, Fisherman's Friend. Like the Rocket, the Train was withdrawn after the Illuminations of 1999.

In 1963, Railcoach 222 was drastically rebuilt into Blackpool's first and only double deck illuminated feature car. The 'Hovertram', numbered 735, seated 99 passengers and resembled a hovercraft with the roof-mounted pods. The resulting low height of the upper deck roof necessitated a sunken gangway. The Hovertram continued in service until after the Illuminations of 2001.

The last of the 'modern' illuminated fleet was built in 1965. Frigate 'HMS Blackpool', numbered 736, was based on the Royal Navy anti-submarine frigate of the same name. Pantograph 170 was stripped to become

Above: **'Standard' 159 is seen here at Pleasure Beach in 1960 advertising the Illuminations for that year. One of a pair specially decorated, they were a popular addition to the illuminated fleet.**
(Andrew Hazlehurst Collection)

Left: **Taken from North Pier in the 1950s, this view of the switch-on shows just how popular the evening is. As well as Talbot Square itself, crowds have filled the roadway and the Promenade on the near side of the tramlines.**

The Blackpool Belle, of 1959, was the first specially built feature car to carry fare-paying passengers. Being twin ended, it could run effectively in either direction. The Belle is seen here before sponsorship was applied.

Following the withdrawal of the 'Blackpool Belle', the Illuminations Department created their own paddle steamer from a converted milk float. Christened the 'Blackpool Queen', it could usually be found playing music on the Promenade between North and Central Piers. It is seen here in 1982.

Seating 95 passengers, the Western Train, seen here in 1996, still has most of its original features, including the working bell on the front. Features that did disappear were the cowcatcher on the front and the smoke machine, which bellowed out smoke into the queues of people wishing to board it!

(Andrew Hazlehurst)

the base of the frigate and its underframe was extended to 52ft. The driver was seated high in a separate cab, but suffered restricted vision, unable to see anybody crossing directly in front of the tram. To overcome this, a very distinctive air hooter was fitted that had the effect of making everybody on the Promenade jump! From 1965, Prudential Assurance sponsored the car, even renaming the tram HMS Prudential in 1980. The Frigate was finally withdrawn from service after the Illuminations of 2001.

January 2001 saw the construction of an Illuminated Trawler. Sponsored by Lofthouses, it was based on the trawler that has been the symbol of Fisherman's Friend for many years. Unlike previous illuminated feature cars, the trawler was designed to run in regular service throughout the year, although not always illuminated! The stripped frame of dismantled tram 633 was fitted with a new underframe and steel-framed ends. Although designed with a bow and stern, the trawler could be driven from either of the two fully fitted cabs. A further specially

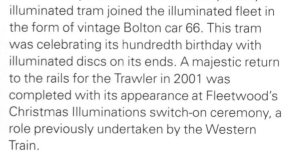

illuminated tram joined the illuminated fleet in the form of vintage Bolton car 66. This tram was celebrating its hundredth birthday with illuminated discs on its ends. A majestic return to the rails for the Trawler in 2001 was completed with its appearance at Fleetwood's Christmas Illuminations switch-on ceremony, a role previously undertaken by the Western Train.

Following the withdrawal of the Hovertram and Frigate, the Trawler was the only member of the illuminated fleet to run in the Illuminations of 2002. It was supplemented by Bolton 66, the restored – but not illuminated – vintage tram, which had had its birthday illuminations re-applied.

Having the distinction of being the only purpose-built double deck feature car, the 'Hovertram' has a high seating capacity of 99. The Blackpool Belle only seated 32 and the Rocket 46.

(Andrew Hazlehurst)

In 1994, 'HMS Blackpool' was decorated to mark Blackpool's 'Festival '94'. The 'two tall stories' were the Tower celebrating its centenary and the new 'Big One' rollercoaster at the Pleasure Beach.

(Andrew Hazlehurst)

The illuminated 'Trawler' of 2001 is the first of the feature cars to appear regularly throughout the year. Fitted with destination blinds and cabs at both ends, it can run in either direction.

(Andrew Hazlehurst)

The 2004 Frigate under construction at Rigby Road tram depot in 2004.

(Andrew Hazlehurst)

In a surprise move, the Western Train made a guest appearance at the annual Tram Sunday transport event at Fleetwood on 20th July 2002. Unable to operate under its own power, the tram was split, towed up separately and repositioned together at Fleetwood Ferry. A further announcement that day by Blackpool Transport was the rebuild of the Frigate for return to use during the 2004 Illuminations. Work was soon started on the tram and a redesigned frame was fitted, incorporating little of the former bodywork. The newly designed body was based loosely on real-life warship HMS Beaver. The tram was fitted with model helicopter, radar, rocket launchers and new – but still loud – horns. Similar to the Trawler it was fitted with destination blinds in order to be used throughout the year, but this time air-conditioning was fitted. The seating capacity is 64 and the new car looks set to be a popular feature in the Illuminations.

13   One vision

Charles Furness
(Photograph by Fred Ash)

Frederick Field
(News Chronicle picture)

Harry Carpenter
(Messrs. Turnbull, Blackpool)

From Lamp to Laser, the Illuminations have come on in leaps and bounds over the years. From the inception of the Illuminations as an annual event in 1912, to the present day, the job of being responsible for the famous display has rested on the shoulders of only eight men.

Charles Furness 1912–1936

Holding the post of Borough Electrical Engineer from 1902-1936, Charles Furness was the man responsible for the original Illuminations displays. Besides his triumph in creating the Illuminations event, he was also responsible for the purchase of new trams and oversaw the integration of the Blackpool and Fleetwood Tramroad Company in 1920. In 1932, a new Transport Manager was appointed to allow Furness and his aide Frederick Field to concentrate on the Illuminations.

Frederick Field 1936–1949

Frederick Field was instrumental in the setting up of the Illuminations Department and Depot, which still exists today. He came to Blackpool as a student of Robert Cornelius Quinn, the then Electrical Engineer for the Borough. After becoming Sub-station Engineer, he worked on the changeover of the tramways from the old promenade to the new. He was later appointed resident Electrical Engineer for the Transport Department, and worked on the re-electrification of the Fleetwood tramline.

Particularly skilled in the field of Illuminations, he helped develop the small-scale display into the nationally-famed spectacle of the time. During the War, he was responsible for the tableaux that were built in front of the Town Hall to promote savings weeks. He retired in 1946, after 47 years service with the Corporation, but was persuaded to return in 1949 to organise the first post-war display.

Harry Carpenter 1950–1974

Born in Blackpool, Harry Carpenter spent all his working life in the lighting industry. He started in 1926, working for the Thornton Cleveleys Electricity Authority. Promoted to Chief Assistant in 1933, he worked his way up to Chief Electrical Engineer and Manager by 1945.

Before taking up the post as Illuminations and Public Street Lighting Officer to the Blackpool Corporation, Harry was the Domestic and Commercial Development Engineer to the North Western Electricity Board. Inheriting electrical equipment and methods which dated from before the War, Harry was responsible for updating all the electrical equipment and the building of substations along the Promenade. Harry retired in 1974, leaving the Illuminations Department in the very capable hands of his deputy Arthur Elliott.

Arthur Elliott.

Arthur Elliott 1974–1988

Joining the Corporation's Electrical Services Department as a Junior Engineer in 1952, Arthur Elliott was promoted to Senior engineer by 1958. For two years he worked in Manchester, but returned in 1960 as Deputy Director, working closely with Harry Carpenter. Following Carpenter's retirement, Arthur was the obvious choice to succeed him, showing the same enthusiasm that Harry had brought to the role.

Arthur carried a small book around with him, jotting down ideas for features as they occurred to him. He also drew inspiration from holidaymakers and residents, mingling with them on the Promenade, overhearing reactions to displays and finding out what they wanted to see. In a television interview he once proudly commented: "The Illuminations are designed by Blackpool people and built by Blackpool people". Arthur retired after the Illuminations of 1988, 36 years after first joining the Department.

Arnold Bennison.

Arnold Bennison 1988–1991

Following Arthur Elliott's retirement, the decision to automatically promote his deputy was not taken and, instead, the Council advertised the post in the press with the slogan 'Put your name in Lights'. The advertisement was answered by Arnold Bennison, who was offered the post of Director of Electrical and Mechanical Services.

Arnold had a Naval background and his appointment was a surprising one, as he had never seen the Illuminations! However, he used his experience in infrastructure to update equipment with new technology. He employed younger engineers who brought new ideas with them. One of these was Richard Ryan, who would later become Illuminations Manager himself.

Frank Hilton.
(The Gazette, Blackpool)

Frank Hilton 1991–1993

Restructuring within Council departments led to Arnold Bennison moving on and the appointment of his deputy, Frank Hilton, to the position of Illuminations Manager.

Frank joined the Department in 1963 as a technician and after serving under Harry Carpenter was promoted to Senior Engineer, becoming Assistant Director in 1983. During his years with the Department he was responsible for introducing electronic controllers and helped produce a section called 'Firework Spectacular', which was the first to be fully operated by electronics.

Naturally, the Blackpool sea air did not take kindly to electronics, so Frank had to come up with an idea for protection. After many sleepless nights and head scratching he thought Tupperware boxes might be the answer, and sure enough they worked very well! Frank retired in 1993.

Keith Hall 1993–1999

Keith first started working for Blackpool Borough Council in 1967, working in the Town Clerk's Department. A qualified engineer and experienced draughtsman he

Keith Hall.

Richard Ryan.

became Illuminations Manager in 1993 and oversaw the complete renewal of Illuminations infrastructure between 1994 and 1998.

During his reign, Keith Hall had a unique system of alerting himself to the possibility of storm damage to the Illuminations. He would use the cherry tree in his front garden; if the winds were blowing and the branches reached a certain angle, Keith knew it was serious enough for him to go and have a drive down the Promenade to check the display for storm damage.

Retiring in 1999 he was succeeded by Richard Ryan.

Richard Ryan 1999–date

Lights have played a part in Richard Ryan's life since the age of six, when he used to watch the Christmas lights going up in his hometown of Sheffield on a Sunday. As he recalled: "Sheffield was definitely my inspiration. We used to come to Blackpool in September as the warm up for Sheffield's Christmas lights!"

The following year he started work on his own illuminated display in his garden, with the aid of his father. At the age of 10 he created his own tableau in the form of a windmill, later adding flashing lights which ran using a potentially lethal 240 Volt live revolving tin can with Meccano contacts. He still has this at his home.

In 1973 and 1974, aged 12, Richard spent his summer holidays doing voluntary work for Matlock Bath Illuminations in Derbyshire. Here he learnt how to coil and connect festoon lighting. His mother subsequently wrote to Arthur Elliott asking how Richard would be able to get a job at Blackpool. Following Arthur's advice, Richard enrolled on an electrical engineering course at Portsmouth Polytechnic. He spent his free time working as a lighting designer in a nightclub and later spent three summer holidays working as a ride operator/electrician at Fun Acres Amusement Park at Southsea.

After leaving Portsmouth with an HND in Electrical and Electronic Engineering, Richard was unable to get a job in the lighting industry as opportunities were thin on the ground.

At the age of 28, he spotted a job advert for Blackpool Illuminations. He didn't get the job he went for but was taken on anyway on the strength of a spectacular portfolio. Richard had landed his dream job. He was initially in charge of the Depot and, within six months, new features." It was an interesting time to land," said Richard. "Arthur Elliot had just retired and Arnold Bennison was just in post. They had previously employed about seven engineers, which was suddenly cut to four, so we were all doing several jobs each. I was young and new in the post, so it was very challenging and a fantastic opportunity".

Following promotion to Senior Engineer, Richard finally made it to Illuminations Manager in 1999. Richard recalls: "I had a total baptism of fire. On my first night in post the water main blew and the Depot was flooded. Within two months we had suffered the worst storms for years and £60,000 worth of lights were spread all over the Promenade. Character building stuff!"

With Richard at the helm, video projections, interactive tableaux, audio tracks, lasers and LED displays have been introduced, and the style of the displays has changed noticeably.

Richard's philosophy is to seek to innovate and yet not alienate traditional Illuminations visitors. He said: "I believe in a mix of tradition and innovation. We must always give customers more than they expect. I hope we surprise them in a positive way."

The stars came out   **14**

Five!... Four!... Three!... Two!... One!...
Every autumn the crowd counts down to the event which has become the number one feature in Blackpool's calendar.

The first night of the Illuminations has always been a big crowd pleaser and, by 1934, the sheer popularity of the show more-or-less demanded an official ceremony to commemorate the start of the annual spectacle. Lord Derby was given the honour of being the first celebrity to perform the official 'Switch-On' and further ceremonies followed before war put a stop to the Lights altogether.

For many years the switch-on ceremony was held outside the Town Hall in Talbot Square and every year the choice of celebrity is a closely guarded secret. Although only a split second event in itself, the switch-on is preceded by several hours of entertainment.

Above: **All ready for the big switch-on, the television trams were fitted with cameras, spotlights, a commentary box and transmitting equipment.** (WGS Hyde)

Left: **The Lights have been switched on by people from all walks of life. House of Commons speaker, Dr. Horace King, took centre stage at the switch-on ceremony in 1967.**

Above left: **Local 'Lassie' Gracie Fields was guest of honour at the 1964 Illuminations.**

Above right: **In 1951, Stanley Matthews performed the switch-on. It became customary to build a miniature tableau relating to the celebrity for display on switch-on night.**

Right: **'Mr Blackpool' himself, Reginald Dixon, threw the big switch in 1956.**

The saying "It'll be alright on the night" had always applied to the famous switch-on ceremonies, particularly since the introduction of rehearsals during the 1950s. For anybody attending the ceremonies, the night can be unforgettable, as was the case in 1974 when Wendy Craig placed a giant plug into a socket to switch on the Lights, triggering a planned explosion under organist Raymond Wallbank, who slumped over his keyboard in mock shock. His acting was so realistic that alarmed guests on the official platform raced to his aid.

Hoping for a problem-free switch-on in 1975, panic soon set in amongst officials when it was found that Doctor Who star Tom Baker had left his 'sonic screwdriver' back in his hotel room. A small sketch involving Cybermen and Daleks had been

The Illuminations switch-on ceremonies have always been popular events, like this one in 1938. Crowds would turn up in all weathers to gather around the stage outside the Town Hall in Talbot Square. More than just somebody flicking a switch, the build up would last for several hours.

planned, so events had to be delayed whilst the prop was retrieved. It was traditional for the guest to hand out sticks of rock to children after the switch-on, but Tom Baker refused to do this, saying that it was bad for their teeth and so was not in keeping with his role. Normal service was resumed in 1976 for the Borough's centenary, at which time there was a big procession along the Promenade. Truth be told though, this was a distinctly watered down affair when compared to similar events in the past.

However, when the Muppets joined Kermit the Frog for the switch-on in 1979, a life-sized Sweetums accidentally knocked the tiara off Miss UK, Carolyn Seaward; an appropriately named lady if ever there was one!

The 50th formal Illuminations display was held in 1982, with a section of golden arches displayed on the carriageway to mark the event. This took place shortly after

Below left: **Switch-on with Shirley Ann Field in 1962.**

Below right: **Wendy Craig prepares to plug in the 1974 Illuminations.**

Above left: **One of Britain's most famous television icons, the Daleks, helped Doctor Who switch on the Lights in 1975. Also seen here is the 1975 'Rail 150' Promenade feature, celebrating 150 years of passenger trains.**

Right: **"Don't panic Mr Mainwaring!". The cast of Dads Army used a mortar to switch on the Illuminations in 1971.**

the Falklands war, task force commander Rear Admiral Sandy Woodward throwing the switch after announcing: "For the 50th time, the Illuminations are switched on. For my second time – let battle commence." Perhaps in this politically correct age he may have been asked to amend his speech!

To make the 50th display more memorable, revolutionary fibre optics and laser beams were added, proving that Blackpool was keen to keep up with the latest technologies. In the case of the lasers, clearance had to be granted from the Civil Aviation Authority, which feared interference with military and civil aircraft, and also from the Health and Safety Executive, which quite naturally was concerned with the crowd's safety. High-powered automated searchlights completed the display.

In 1989, Frank Bruno – the ever-popular boxer and wit – turned on the Lights. However, the customary open top tour of the Illuminations was not as enjoyable as usual due to a massive downpour, and this most definitely was not a case of "alright 'arry!"

The shortest-lived Illuminations took place on switch-on night in 1992, when the Lights were only on for less than one minute. It appears that the actual switch itself only controlled the section adjacent to the Town Hall and, prior to computerisation, members of staff would switch on the other sections manually – systematically – along the Promenade. Just ten minutes before Lisa Stansfield was due to turn on the Lights, a roadie accidentally hit the switch; when staff at the adjacent sections saw the lights go on they immediately turned theirs on too, consequently within seconds

all six miles of the display were fully lit. Fortunately though many staff had radios and so the rather embarrassing message to turn the Lights off was quickly given.

This wasn't the only time things didn't go to plan that year. A new tableau called 'Rockin' Petals' featured two flowers which danced to a karaoke machine. To complete the lifelike disco experience, a smoke machine was fitted, but this brought about phone calls to the fire brigade from concerned motorists claiming the tableau was on fire! A sign was then placed prominently on the front saying, "This feature is designed to smoke." Unfortunately it couldn't be clearly read from the road and so the emergency calls were still being made, causing the fire brigade to get rather hot under the collar. A rather sheepish Illuminations Department eventually reacted and quietly removed the offending smoke machine.

For the 2002 Illuminations a decision was made to move the switch-on ceremony to the car park behind the Golden Mile. It was felt that this was a safer venue, off the Promenade, where larger crowds could be catered for. The Radio 2 Arena now hosts an impressive line up of pop stars, lasers and other lighting effects to delight the crowds. The evening is usually transmitted live across the nation and now globally with the Internet.

A full list of the celebrities who have switched on the lights can be found on page 132.

Earl and Countess Spencer performed the switch-on in 1981.

The cast of Coronation Street were asked to switch on the Lights using beer pumps in 1983.

Dates of the Illuminations and the Switch-On Personalities

1912				14 days	
1913	18th Sep	to	18th Oct	31 days	
1925	26th Sep	to	24th Oct	29 days	
1926	25th Sep	to	23rd Oct	29 days	
1927	24th Sep	to	24th Oct	31 days	
1928	22nd Sep	to	22nd Oct	31 days	
1929	21st Sep	to	21st Oct	31 days	
1930	20th Sep	to	20th Oct	31 days	
1931	19th Sep	to	19th Oct	31 days	
1932	24th Sep	to	24th Oct	31 days	
1933	16th Sep	to	23rd Oct	38 days	
1934	15th Sep	to	22nd Oct	38 days	Lord Derby
1935	14th Sep	to	21st Oct	38 days	Audrey Mosson (Railway Queen)
1936	12th Sep	to	19th Oct	38 days	Sir Josiah Stamp
1937	18th Sep	to	25th Oct	38 days	Alderman Ashton (later Duke of Kent)
1938	16th Sep	to	24th Oct	39 days	Councillor Mrs. Quayle
1939	15th Sep	to	23rd Oct	39 days	(cancelled)
1949	16th Sep	to	24th Oct	39 days	Anna Neagle
1950	15th Sep	to	23rd Oct	39 days	Wilfred Pickles
1951	6th Sep	to	22nd Oct	47 days	Stanley Matthews
1952	4th Sep	to	20th Oct	47 days	Valerie Hobson
1953	9th Sep	to	20th Oct	48 days	George Formby
1954	10th Sep	to	25th Oct	46 days	Gilbert Harding
1955	9th Sep	to	26th Oct	48 days	Russian Ambassador Jacob Malik
1956	5th Sep	to	22nd Oct	48 days	Reginald Dixon
1957	6th Sep	to	21st Oct	46 days	American Ambassador John H Whitney
1958	3rd Sep	to	20th Oct	48 days	'Matty' Matthews
1959	5th Sep	to	19th Oct	45 days	Jayne Mansfield
1960	2nd Sep	to	17th Oct	46 days	Janet Munro
1961	8th Sep	to	29th Oct	52 days	Violet Carson
1962	7th Sep	to	28th Oct	52 days	Shirley Ann Field
1963	6th Sep	to	27th Oct	52 days	Cliff Michelmore

1964	4th Sep	to	25th Oct	52 days	Gracie Fields
1965	3rd Sep	to	24th Oct	52 days	David Tomlinson
1966	2nd Sep	to	23rd Oct	52 days	Ken Dodd
1967	8th Sep	to	29th Oct	52 days	Dr. Horace King
1968	6th Sep	to	27th Oct	52 days	Sir Matt Busby
1969	5th Sep	to	26th Oct	52 days	RAF/Battle of Britain
1970	4th Sep	to	25th Oct	52 days	Tony Blackburn
1971	3rd Sep	to	24th Oct	52 days	Dad's Army cast
1972	8th Sep	to	29th Oct	52 days	Danny La Rue
1973	7th Sep	to	28th Oct	52 days	Gordon Banks
1974	6th Sep	to	27th Oct	52 days	Wendy Craig
1975	5th Sep	to	26th Oct	52 days	Dr. Who cast
1976	3rd Sep	to	31st Oct	59 days	Miss U.K Carol Ann Grant
1977	2nd Sep	to	30th Oct	59 days	Red Rum and Red Arrows
1978	1st Sep	to	29th Oct	59 days	Terry Wogan
1979	31st Aug	to	28th Oct	59 days	Kermit The Frog
1980	28th Aug	to	26th Oct	60 days	Cannon and Ball
1981	4th Sep	to	1st Nov	59 days	Earl & Countess Spencer
1982	3rd Sep	to	31st Oct	59 days	Rear Admiral J.F. Woodward
1983	26th Aug	to	30th Oct	66 days	Coronation Street cast
1984	24th Aug	to	28th Oct	66 days	Johannes Rau, Prime Minister of North Rhine/Westphalia and David Waddington QC, MP, Minister of State, Home Office
1985	30th Aug	to	27th Oct	59 days	Joanna Lumley and BBC Children In Need
1986	5th Sep	to	2nd Nov	59 days	Les Dawson
1987	4th Sep	to	1st Nov	59 days	BBC Holiday Programme
1988	2nd Sep	to	6th Nov	66 days	Andrew Lloyd Webber & Sarah Brightman
1989	1st Sep	to	5th Nov	66 days	Frank Bruno
1990	31st Aug	to	5th Nov	67 days	Julie Goodyear & Roy Barraclough
1991	30th Aug	to	3rd Nov	66 days	Judith Chalmers and Derek Jameson
1992	4th Sep	to	8th Nov	66 days	Lisa Stansfield
1993	3rd Sep	to	7th Nov	66 days	Status Quo and Radio One
1994	2nd Sep	to	6th Nov	66 days	Shirley Bassey
1995	1st Sep	to	5th Nov	66 days	Bee Gees and Radio One
1996	30th Aug	to	3rd Nov	66 days	Eternal and Radio One
1997	29th Aug	to	2nd Nov	66 days	Michael Ball and Radio Two
1998	4th Sep	to	8th Nov	66 days	Chris De Burgh and Radio Two
1999	3rd Sep	to	7th Nov	66 days	Gary Barlow and Radio Two
2000	1st Sep	to	12th Nov	69 days	Westlife and Radio Two
2001	31st Aug	to	4th Nov	66 days	Steps and Radio Two
2002	30th Aug	to	3rd Nov	66 days	Ronan Keating and Radio Two
2003	29th Aug	to	2nd Nov	66 days	Blue and Radio Two
2004	3rd Sep	to	7th Nov	66 days	

Suggested further reading

Abell, PH & McLoughlin, I: 'Blackpool Trams – The First Half Century 1885 – 1932', 1997

Barritt, S: 'The Black Pool of 1788'

Bennett, P: 'Blackpool Pleasure Beach : A Century of Fun', 1996

Bonney, D: 'Blackpool under Fire'

Clarke, A: 'Windmill Land', 1916

Cunliffe, N: 'Aspects of Blackpool's History', 1997

Curtis, B: 'Blackpool Tower', 1988

Dobson, B: 'Blackpool and Fleetwood a Century Ago', 1991

Eyre, K: 'Seven Golden Miles: The Fantastic Story of Blackpool', 1961

Porter, J: 'History of the Fylde of Lancashire', 1976

Readers Digest, 'Journeys into the Past: Life On The Home Front', 1996

Rothwell, C: 'Bright and Breezy Blackpool', 1991

Turner, B: 'Circular Tour – Seaside Pleasure Riding By Tram', 1999

Turner, B & Palmer, S: 'The Blackpool Story', 1976 (reprinted 1994)

Wood, A & Lightbown, T: 'Blackpool in old Picture Postcards, Vols 1 & 2', 1983/1990

Iluminations staff, pictured at the Depot in 2004.